JAMES MONROE

PRESIDENTIAL ✧ LEADERS

JAMES MONROE

DEBBIE LEVY

LERNER PUBLICATIONS COMPANY / MINNEAPOLIS

A NOTE ABOUT SPELLINGS: Most people of James Monroe's era spelled words quite differently than we do. They also used different grammar and capitalization. This book preserves the original spelling and punctuation of all historical writings.

In memory of my father, Harold Levy, 1913–2003

Lerner Publications Company
A division of Lerner Publishing Group
241 First Avenue North
Minneapolis, MN 55401 U.S.A.

Website address: www.lernerbooks.com

Library of Congress Cataloging-in-Publication Data

Levy, Debbie.
James Monroe / Debbie Levy.
p. cm. — (Presidential leaders)
Includes bibliographical references (p.) and index.
Contents: Revolutionary roots—Soldier to politician—A thankless mission—Governor Monroe—Jefferson's man in Europe—Seasoned leader—The fifth president—Times of change—Winding down.
ISBN: 0-8225-0824-9 (lib. bdg. : alk. paper)
1. Monroe, James, 1758–1831—Juvenile literature. 2. Presidents—United States—Biography—Juvenile literature. [1. Monroe, James, 1758–1831. 2. Presidents.] I. Title. II. Series.
E372.L485 2005
973.5'4'092—dc22 2003023643

Manufactured in the United States of America
1 2 3 4 5 6 – JR – 10 09 08 07 06 05

CONTENTS

James Monroe became acting secretary of war in December 1812. Although he did his best to improve the U.S. military system, the War of 1812 against Great Britain ended without a clear winner.

INTRODUCTION

You had better make preparations to leave.

—Secretary of State James Monroe to President James Madison, August 23, 1814, as Monroe discovered British troops marching toward Washington, D.C.

Almost as soon as Congress declared war on Great Britain in June 1812, the United States started losing it. The war effort lacked money, and both the U.S. Army and Navy were outmatched by their British counterparts. In early 1813, President James Madison appointed a New Yorker named John Armstrong to be secretary of war. Madison hoped Armstrong would organize U.S. forces and come up with plans for turning around the failing U.S. war effort. But then a fleet of British warships gathered in Maryland's Chesapeake Bay in the spring of 1813. Armstrong dismissed the concerns of a fellow member of the cabinet (a group of presidential advisers) that the enemy might attack Washington, D.C., the nation's capital. When British ships massed in the Potomac River just downstream from the capital in July 1813, that same cabinet member proposed ways to strengthen Washington's defenses. Armstrong again disagreed. When the cabinet member advised forming a communications system throughout the Chesapeake region, to provide leaders in Washington with news of enemy movements, Armstrong nixed that idea as well.

Who was the cabinet member offering all this unwanted advice? It was James Monroe, the secretary of state. A hero and military officer during the American Revolution (1775–1783), Monroe had more firsthand experience with war than any other member of Madison's cabinet. But as secretary of state, Monroe's job was to advise the president on matters of diplomacy—how to deal peacefully with other countries. His job was not to offer war strategies. Madison chose to listen to Armstrong's belief that the British were no threat to the capital.

A year later, British ships again gathered at the mouth of the Potomac. The British military's exact plans were a mystery to U.S. leaders, who had failed to create the communications chain that Monroe had proposed. But Monroe's prediction of an attack on the capital appeared to be coming true, and President Madison finally turned to him for advice and action. Monroe led a small group of soldiers out of Washington to gather information. He found the British about fifty miles away in Maryland. They were preparing for an overland attack on the capital. Other British soldiers were sailing up the Potomac, also in the direction of Washington.

Monroe worked tirelessly, riding from one point to another, tracking the British and sending messengers to inform Madison and others of the changing situation. But it was too late to make up for the Americans' lack of preparation. On August 24, 1814, the British easily crushed a force of American militia (citizen soldiers) at Bladensburg, Maryland, just outside the capital.

The invaders moved toward Washington. U.S. leaders realized that the small force assigned to defend Washington would not be able to drive away the British. The leaders urged the city's citizens to flee to the countryside. Monroe stayed in the capital until the citizens and any remaining troops had departed. On the night of August 24, Monroe left for Virginia as well, and the British marched into an empty Washington.

Monroe went only as far as a private home across the Potomac from the city. From there, he could see Washington burning. The British set fire to one public building after another—the U.S. Capitol, the president's mansion, the Department of State. Only weather saved the city from total destruction, as massive thunderstorms rained down soon after the invasion. The British left the smoldering city on August 25, a day after they had arrived.

After the invasion of Washington, John Armstrong left his post as secretary of war in disgrace. Madison appointed Monroe to be both secretary of war and secretary of state. Monroe created the military communications system—a group of express horseback riders—he had wanted to build the year before. He raised salaries for U.S. soldiers to try to attract more volunteers. He organized the armed forces' supply system. Monroe was not entirely successful, but the Americans did manage to push the British out of nearby Baltimore, Maryland, and to score victories in battles near Canada.

The War of 1812 ended in a draw, with neither nation a victor. But the conflict produced at least one winner: Monroe. Only a few years earlier, his reputation as a political leader had been marred by his own mistakes, by political fighting, and by situations beyond his control. But his wartime devotion to duty restored his good political name and polished it to a high gloss. In 1816, his reputation glowing from the recent war, Monroe was elected the fifth president of the United States.

CHAPTER ONE

REVOLUTIONARY ROOTS

He has in every instance maintained the reputation of a brave, active and sensible officer.

—General George Washington, in 1779, describing twenty-one-year-old Major James Monroe

If geography determines a person's destiny, then the baby Elizabeth Monroe bore on April 28, 1758, was a born leader. Elizabeth and her husband, Spence Monroe, lived in the Tidewater are of Virginia, between the Potomac and Rappahannock rivers. The families of this region produced some of the most famous leaders of the early days of the United States. These families included the Washingtons (whose son George became the first president), the Madisons (whose son James became the fourth president), and the Marshalls (whose son John became the fourth chief justice of the U.S. Supreme Court).

But of course, a person's future is not controlled by geography alone, and the Monroes' baby boy—whom they named James—could have been destined to the life of a poor farmer. The once-rich soil of Tidewater was exhausted after years of cultivation. Spence Monroe owned five hundred acres, which was not a very large farm compared to other families. Using slave labor, Spence raised tobacco—a crop that only worsened the condition of the soil.

Little is known about James's childhood. He was the oldest boy in the family, with three brothers and a sister. When not learning the business of farming, James spent hours roaming the countryside, shooting rabbits and squirrels for the family's table. The Monroes were not part of Tidewater's wealthy society, which indulged in parties and fine dinners.

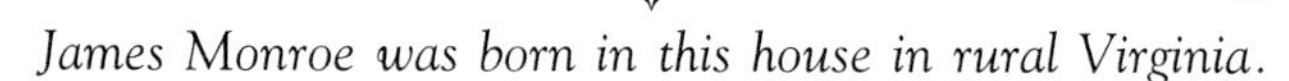

James Monroe was born in this house in rural Virginia.

Still, the Monroes were involved in the major events of their day. Virginia was one of the thirteen colonies in British America. By the time James was born, colonists were rebelling against rules imposed by Great Britain. In need of money after years of European wars, the British government raised funds by taxing the American colonies. When Americans purchased tea or newspapers, for example, they had to pay taxes and duties to the British government. Colonists objected because they did not want to pay high fees on everyday items. But they also objected because they did not have a voice in the government that made these decisions. American colonists could not elect people to send to Great Britain to represent their needs and desires.

James's father admired Patrick Henry, a patriot (as anti-British colonists came to be known) who made fiery speeches against Great Britain. James's uncle, Judge Joseph Jones, was a good friend of George Washington, James Madison, and Thomas Jefferson and, like them, was a leader of Virginia patriots. As patriots around him embraced the idea of an independent American nation, young James listened and observed.

TIMES OF TURMOIL

In 1769, at the age of eleven, James started school. James and his friend John Marshall walked together to the all-boy Campbelltown Academy each day. John, the future Supreme Court justice, was brainy even as a boy. James may not have been as brilliant as his friend, but he was a good student, especially in math and Latin.

During James's school days, the patriots' complaints grew louder. In March 1770, British troops in Boston,

Paul Revere's engraving of the Boston Massacre (above) *is an inaccurate depiction of the event. In fact, the British troops had been cornered by a mob that outnumbered them.*

Massachusetts, fired into a group of colonists who were harassing the soldiers. Five colonists were killed. Boston patriot Samuel Adams condemned the soldiers' actions as the "Boston Massacre." He urged colonists to revolt.

In December 1773, a group of colonists boarded three British ships docked in Boston Harbor and dumped hundreds of crates of valuable tea overboard. To punish the patriots for this act of protest—dubbed the Boston Tea Party—British officials closed the port of Boston to shipping.

They also restricted public meetings in Massachusetts. Throughout the colonies, patriots protested the British reaction by declaring June 1, 1774, a day of fasting and prayer.

Leaders of the patriots had also begun organizing the First Continental Congress in Philadelphia, Pennsylvania. Members of the Congress discussed their objections to Great Britain's treatment of the colonies. Revolution was in the air.

As things moved toward a crisis between the colonists and Great Britain, James suffered a sad loss. In 1774 both of his parents died within months of each other. As the oldest boy in the family, James was expected to take over as head of the household. Fortunately, Uncle Joseph helped James run the farm and supervised the children's education.

James was sixteen, old enough to go to college. He planned to attend the College of William and Mary in Williamsburg, Virginia, but his parents' deaths cast a shadow on that plan. Uncle Joseph encouraged James to go after all. So in August 1774, the newly orphaned teenager—a tall, strongly built country boy—rode into Virginia's bustling capital city and registered at the College of William and Mary.

CLAMOR ON CAMPUS

As a student, Monroe did not make much of a mark at William and Mary, except for one episode. In the spring of 1775, Monroe joined a small group of students who signed a petition complaining about Maria Digges. Digges was the "Mistress of the College," responsible for the living quarters at the college. The petition complained that Digges served bad food, neglected students when they fell sick, sold college supplies for her own profit, and was rude.

James enrolled at the College of William and Mary in August 1774. During his time there, he became involved in the revolutionary cause.

College professors held a hearing on the petition. But Monroe did not contribute much to the hearing. He had merely followed the lead of the others and had to admit—presumably to his embarrassment—"[t]hat he had never read the petition and consequently could not undertake to prove a single article."

Soon Monroe and the other students had more serious matters on their minds. On April 19, 1775, American militia clashed with British troops in two small Massachusetts towns, Lexington and Concord. The American Revolution had begun. News of the start of the war reached Williamsburg in late April 1775, just as Monroe celebrated his seventeenth birthday. Rallying to the revolutionary cause, he immediately joined a company of volunteer student soldiers.

With his skill with a gun and his sturdy good health, Monroe had the makings of a fine soldier. He soon proved that he also had the daring for bold action. As patriots took up arms throughout Virginia, the British royal governor, Lord Dunmore, fled Williamsburg. On June 24, 1775, a group of patriots burst into his palace, where servants still worked. The patriots had heard that Lord Dunmore had stashed weapons in the palace. They found 230 muskets, 301 swords, and 18 pistols. They took the arms to a storage building for safekeeping. Among the two dozen men who carried out this mission, the youngest was seventeen-year-old Monroe.

On July 3, 1775, George Washington was given command of the patriots' new Continental Army (known as the Continentals), created by the Continental Congress. On September 28, 1775, Monroe volunteered as a lieutenant for a Virginia regiment of the army. His outfit, the Third Virginia Regiment of Foot, trained in Williamsburg. On July 4, 1776, the Continental Congress made its Declaration of Independence. It declared that the American colonies were free from British rule. Shortly after that, Monroe and his friends received their orders. The Virginians were needed six hundred miles away in New York.

FIGHTING IN NEW YORK

In early August 1776, the seven hundred men of Virginia's Third Regiment started the long trek north. Monroe and the others marched for a month in the summer's heat. On September 3, the Virginians met up with Washington's troops at Harlem Heights, at the northern tip of Manhattan island, in New York City. By that time, the British had already taken Long Island, off the coast of

New York. Washington and his soldiers were thrilled to see new arrivals. The Virginia regiments seemed well trained and eager to fight. Washington's army, which was made up of poorly supplied volunteers, was ragtag and had lost many soldiers.

The Virginians increased the Continentals' fighting strength, but the revolutionary army was still weak. When the British invaded New York City in mid-September, many of the city's defenders simply ran away. But when the British pushed northward through Manhattan, they encountered the Virginia soldiers and others, who held the rocky hills of Harlem. The Battle of Harlem Heights was Monroe's first experience on the front lines of battle.

HEROISM IN TRENTON

Monroe's next New York battle was at the end of October 1776, in White Plains. There, the Americans inflicted heavy losses on the British. But the ranks of the Continental Army were thin, and winter was approaching. Washington tried to recruit more troops, but few men wanted to join the struggling army.

Finally, in early December, Washington retreated with his soldiers, including the Virginia regiments, to Trenton, New Jersey. Many became sick on the long, cold march. By the time they arrived in Trenton, only two hundred healthy men were left. Monroe was one of the healthy ones. From Trenton, with the enemy on their heels, the Americans boarded boats and crossed the Delaware River into Pennsylvania. They took with them all their equipment and all the boats.

The enemy included Hessian mercenaries. The British were paying these soldiers from part of present-day Germany to fight. Without boats, the Hessians could not pursue the Americans. The commander of the Hessian troops, Colonel Johann Gottlieb Rall, settled into Trenton. He planned to wait for the Delaware to ice over later in the winter. Then he would cross the solid river into Pennsylvania and attack Philadelphia. But Washington came up with a plan of his own, and Monroe was an important part of it.

Washington's plan was to cross the Delaware again, using the boats his soldiers had gathered, and take the Hessians by surprise. On the night of December 25, 1776, American soldiers set off across the semi-frozen river. Snow was falling in a brisk wind. Blocks of ice knocked into the crowded boats. Boats crossed and recrossed the river, until all 2,400 Continentals were on the New Jersey shore.

Once across, Monroe led a small squad of soldiers ahead to stand guard at an important road junction. But Monroe and his men attracted the attention of a local resident, Dr. Riker. "He came out in the dark to learn the cause [of the commotion], and encountered my command," Monroe wrote later, "and supposing we were from the British camp ordered us off. . . . When he discovered that we were American soldiers, he insisted that we should go to this house, and not stay out in the storm, and he would give us something to eat. I told him my orders were strict and we could not leave, when he returned to the house and brought us some victuals [food]. He said to me, 'I know something is to be done, and I am going with you. I am a doctor, and I may help some poor fellow.' When orders came for us to hasten to Trenton, the doctor went with me."

In the early hours of December 26, the Americans moved on Trenton. The Hessian soldiers had spent

Hessian troops line up to surrender to American forces after the Battle of Trenton.

Christmas feasting and drinking. After their day of celebrating, they were sleeping soundly. The American attack caught them completely by surprise. As they awoke, the Hessians tried to organize a defense. Critical to that defense were two large cannons, sitting untended in the street. The Hessians scrambled to aim the cannons at the oncoming Americans. But Monroe and Captain William Washington hurried to beat the enemy to the guns.

With bullets firing around them, the two Americans captured the cannons. Both men were seriously injured, Monroe by a musket ball in his shoulder. Fortunately, Riker had kept his promise to accompany the American soldiers on their offensive. If he had not been there to provide immediate treatment, Monroe likely would have bled to death.

Rall died in the Battle of Trenton, and his soldiers were badly defeated. For the Americans, the importance of the battle was not simply that they drove the Hessians out of Trenton. The victory raised the spirits of the soldiers and other patriots.

YEARNING FOR ACTION

After further treatment of his wound, Monroe spent more than two months recovering. For his bravery, he was promoted to captain. However, because too few soldiers enlisted in the Continental Army, he did not receive a company to command.

Monroe signed up as an aide to General William Alexander. In 1777 Monroe fought in battles at Brandywine Creek and Germantown, Pennsylvania, and was promoted to major. He spent the harsh winter of 1777–1778 in miserable conditions camped at Valley Forge, Pennsylvania, with the Continental Army. More than two thousand American soldiers died at Valley Forge that winter, struck down by typhus, dysentery, and pneumonia.

The misery of Valley Forge seemed only to intensify Monroe's yearning for more action. He served at the Battle of Monmouth, New Jersey, in the summer of 1778. He scouted enemy movements for George Washington, but this, too, did not provide enough action for the restless soldier. In December 1778, twenty-year-old Monroe retired from the Continental Army.

CRAVING A COMMAND

Monroe was not giving up his desire to lead men in battle. The war's fighting was shifting southward, and Monroe hoped to find a command back in Virginia. To bolster his chances, Monroe obtained a letter of recommendation from General Washington. The commander of the Continental Army addressed his letter to an important member of the Virginia legislature.

Washington's words carried weight. The Virginia legislature was happy to appoint Monroe lieutenant colonel of a regiment. But it could not provide the men for the regiment. If he wanted to command soldiers, Monroe had to find them. As in the Continental Army, Virginia had too many officers and too few regular soldiers. By the end of 1779, Monroe still lacked the command he craved and lacked direction in his life.

BEFRIENDING JEFFERSON

George Washington's recommendation did not produce the command Monroe wanted, but it did help create another opportunity. With advice from his uncle Joseph, Monroe applied to study law with Thomas Jefferson. Although Jefferson was governor of Virginia, he still accepted some law students, and the applicant with a letter of praise from Washington got his attention. He took on Monroe as a new student in 1780.

Before long, Monroe and Jefferson were good friends. Jefferson was fifteen years older than Monroe, but he enjoyed the younger man's company, and he trusted him. As for Monroe, he found in Jefferson a brilliant mentor (counselor). They discussed politics, farming, and countless other subjects. When the capital of Virginia moved from Williamsburg to Richmond, Monroe followed his teacher there. This friendship marked a new beginning in Monroe's life.

CHAPTER TWO

FROM SOLDIER TO POLITICIAN

It gives me pleasure that your county has been wise enough to enlist your talents into their service.

—Thomas Jefferson to James Monroe, May 20, 1782, upon Monroe's election to Virginia's House of Delegates

Against great odds—and with assistance from France—the American revolutionaries defeated the British army at Yorktown, Virginia, on October 19, 1781. Two years later, Great Britain recognized the independent nation of the United States of America by signing the Treaty of Paris.

By the time the treaty was signed, the new nation was organized under the Articles of Confederation. The articles created a weak central, or federal, government, without a president or a court system. The main component of the new government was the Confederation Congress, a one-house legislature with representatives from each of the thirteen states.

After studying with Jefferson, Monroe became a lawyer, but he was not very interested in arguing cases in court. He was far more interested in the new laws being created by the government.

In the spring of 1782, Monroe was elected to the Virginia House of Delegates in Richmond. The House of Delegates was one of two chambers (parts) of the state legislature, or assembly. Monroe allied himself with Virginians such as James Madison and George Mason, who believed the government created by the Articles of Confederation was too weak. They wanted to give the federal government more powers. Leading the opposition to this group was Patrick Henry, who distrusted a strong federal government. Henry, like many Americans, thought that each state should have more power over its own business.

POLITICAL BEGINNINGS

Monroe made an impression on his fellow delegates. In 1783 they selected him as one of Virginia's representatives to the Confederation Congress in Annapolis, Maryland.

Congressional delegates reflected the division in the new country over the meaning of nationhood. Federalists wanted a stronger central government, and antifederalists wanted individual states to be the centers of power. Monroe sided with the federalists, but he took a middle-of-the-road view on many issues. In his first session at the Congress, he stayed on the sidelines of most debates.

A young man of twenty-five, Monroe enjoyed his stay in Annapolis. The town was a center of culture, with theater performances, parties, and horse racing. Monroe shared lodgings with Jefferson, another of Virginia's congressional delegates. They ate dinners together, prepared by Jefferson's French chef. Monroe also enjoyed using Jefferson's private library. Through Jefferson, Monroe became close to Madison. The friendship among the three men would last throughout their lives.

After the Confederation Congress adjourned in June 1784, Monroe traveled westward to see the country. His trip took him north of the Ohio River, where the British still held military posts and where some Native American groups threatened travelers who ventured onto their lands. The trip by horseback and coaches was dangerous and difficult, but Monroe seemed to enjoy it. "I will certainly see all that my time will admit of," he wrote to Jefferson. "It is possible I may lose my scalp from the temper of the Indians but if either a little fighting or a great deal of running will save it, I shall escape safe."

CONFEDERATION CONGRESSMAN

The next session of the Confederation Congress began in October 1784 in Trenton, New Jersey. Monroe was more comfortable speaking up. He argued that the Congress needed the power to regulate commerce (the buying, selling, and transporting of goods) between the states and with foreign nations. But too many people feared giving the federal government too much control, or they were satisfied with things as they were. The Congress did not embrace Monroe's ideas. The expansion of the government's powers would have to wait.

A Founding Friendship

Even Founding Fathers need friends. Perhaps it is not surprising, then, that three of the men who shaped the early history of the United States—James Monroe, James Madison, and Thomas Jefferson—became the best of friends.

Monroe was the youngest of the trio, but he was not merely a junior partner in the friendship. When introducing Monroe to Madison in 1783, Jefferson said of Monroe, "The scrupulousness of his honor will make you safe in the most confidential communications. A better man cannot be."

Among them, Monroe, Madison, and Jefferson held an impressive array of government posts. Monroe had been state legislator, state governor, U.S. senator, minister to France and Great Britain, secretary of state, secretary of war, and president. Madison served as state legislator, congressman, secretary of state, and president. Jefferson had been state legislator, state governor, minister to France, secretary of state, vice president, and president. Each was also responsible for an important document in the nation's formation or

Monroe remained lifelong friends with both Thomas Jefferson (left) *and James Madison* (right).

development: the Declaration of Independence (Jefferson), the Constitution (Madison), and the Monroe Doctrine (Monroe).

Throughout their careers, the three men corresponded frequently about matters both public and personal. As president, Monroe often consulted with Madison and Jefferson, both of whom had held that office before him. In confidential communications, the friends wrote in code, using numbers to represent words, letters, or letter combinations.

But this was not merely a professional association among politicians. Monroe, Madison, and Jefferson shared their everyday lives. When Monroe returned to Virginia in 1797 after serving as minister to France, James and Dolley Madison knew that their friends needed food for their first winter home in three years. Dolley gave the Monroes her own preserved fruits and vegetables, and Madison shared his seed potatoes so the Monroes might grow a crop the following spring. When the Monroes returned to France in 1803, they returned the favor by shopping for household goods for the Madisons, buying them French carpets, curtains, and other items.

As with most relationships, there were rough spots. But the friendship among the three men survived, lasting until the ends of their lives. Jefferson died first, on July 4, 1826. A few years later, Monroe and Madison, both elderly and unwell, realized that they might never see each other again. In the spring of 1831, Monroe wrote to Madison that such a "final separation is among the most distressing incidents which could occur." Madison responded, "The pain I feel at the idea [of not seeing Monroe again], associated as it is with a recollection of the long, close, and uninterrupted friendship which united us, amounts to a pang which I cannot well express." These were the last letters the friends exchanged.

After the 1784–1785 session of Congress, Monroe traveled westward again, this time visiting Kentucky, where he owned land. He learned how much settlers on the western frontier relied on the Mississippi River. Many settlers made their living by selling crops back east. Traveling overland with their goods was difficult and time-consuming. It was much faster to take boats down the Mississippi River to the Gulf of Mexico and, from there, to the East Coast. But Spain controlled the lower reaches of the Mississippi, and the settlers were at Spain's mercy over whether they could use the river freely and safely. Monroe discovered that the settlers were frustrated with the U.S. government, which seemed to ignore their concerns about Spanish control of their lifeline to the rest of the nation.

Monroe's sympathy for the western settlers influenced his work in the next session of the Congress, which began in the fall of 1785 in New York City. U.S. secretary of foreign affairs John Jay and Don Diego de Gardoqui, Spain's minister to the United States, proposed a treaty. Under the treaty, Spain would grant the United States special trade favors if the United States recognized Spain's right to rule the Mississippi. Fresh from his trip to the region that would be most harmed by the deal, Monroe led the fight against the Jay-Gardoqui Treaty. Although powerful people supported the pact, Monroe managed to derail it. The United States did not give up its claims to use the Mississippi.

After serving three one-year terms in the Confederation Congress, Monroe was ready for a break. He was worried about the country's survival, as he believed the Articles of Confederation had created an unworkable system. Without a stronger national government, he feared, the states would squabble and divide. "It has been," he wrote to

Monroe met his future bride, Elizabeth, in 1785.

Jefferson in 1786, "a year of excessive labor & fatigue & unprofitably so."

LAWYER AND FAMILY MAN

Not everything about Monroe's final session with the Confederation Congress was discouraging. During his stay in New York, Monroe met Elizabeth Kortright.

Elizabeth was ten years younger than Monroe and was known for her great beauty and fine clothes. Her family had once been wealthy, but her father had lost his fortune during the revolution. The teenage beauty and the southern gentleman may not have seemed a natural match, but they fell in love. They were married on February 16, 1786. Elizabeth was seventeen, and Monroe was just shy of his twenty-eighth birthday.

After three years as a poorly paid congressman, Monroe needed to earn money. He decided to return to Virginia to practice law. The life of a lawyer held little appeal for him, but he realized that it was the best way to build his bank

Monroe practiced law in this building while living in Fredericksburg, Virginia. The building has been turned into a museum.

account. On October 13, 1786, the Monroes left New York for Fredericksburg, Virginia.

As a country lawyer, Monroe traveled frequently to courts in nearby counties and in Richmond. He did not enjoy his work. But at home, Monroe had reason to be happy, as he wrote to Jefferson: "Mrs. Monroe hath added a daughter to our society who tho' noisy, contributes greatly to its amus'ment." Eliza Monroe was born on December 5, 1786.

CONSIDERING THE CONSTITUTION

In the spring of 1787, Monroe was elected again to Virginia's House of Delegates. The talk in Richmond, where the assembly met, was of the upcoming convention in Philadelphia. Delegates from every state were to meet to consider changing the Articles of Confederation. Monroe hoped his fellow legislators would choose him to be a delegate to the Philadelphia Convention, but they did not.

The fifty–five members of the Philadelphia Convention produced a new Constitution of the United States, to replace the Articles of Confederation. Monroe and other members of the Virginia Assembly studied the proposed Constitution carefully. Its strongest critics disagreed with its strengthening of the federal government. But Monroe found fault with the Constitution in the opposite direction. In his view, the Philadelphia Convention had failed to create a federal government that was powerful enough. He also

George Washington (behind desk) *looks on as delegates sign the new U.S. Constitution.*

objected to the Constitution because it did not contain a bill of rights guaranteeing specific freedoms to individuals.

Edmund Randolph

On June 2, 1788, 173 of Virginia's most influential leaders gathered to ratify (accept) or reject the proposed Constitution. Monroe's former schoolmate John Marshall and Governor Edmund Randolph were there. James Madison, the key architect of the proposed new system of government, also attended. These men all favored the proposed Constitution and approved of the stronger federal government it created. The famous Virginia patriot, Patrick Henry, also served as a delegate. He opposed the proposed new federal powers and became a leading antifederalist.

Monroe was a delegate to the Virginia ratifying convention. He voted against the proposed Constitution, but he was in the minority. Virginia ratified the Constitution by a vote of 89 to 79. By 1788 nine states had ratified the Constitution, enough for it to come into effect under the rules decided at the Philadelphia Convention. By May 1790, all the states of the Union had joined in accepting the Constitution.

LOSING TO MADISON

Monroe was disappointed in this outcome, but he was not terribly upset. He corresponded with Jefferson and Madison as usual and turned his attention back to his law practice. Monroe was also cheered in 1788 by his purchase of a farm in Albemarle County, Virginia, close to Jefferson's home at Monticello. Financially, Monroe was struggling. But he bought his cherished piece of land in Albemarle by a barter arrangement, in which the seller accepted some of Monroe's Kentucky lands as payment.

The autumn of 1788 brought elections for the two parts of the new U.S. Congress—the Senate and the House of Representatives. Monroe was busy with his legal practice, his new farm, and the Virginia House of Delegates. Running for Congress was not in his plan. But James Madison was running for the House of Representatives, and some antifederalists, led by Patrick Henry, wanted to keep him out of the new government. They urged Monroe to run against his friend, and surprisingly, Monroe agreed. Madison won by a large percentage of the total votes.

The campaign did not cause a breach between Monroe and Madison. As Monroe explained in a letter, he had only run because he wished to contribute "my feeble efforts" to the new government, not because he was out to beat Madison. Madison and Jefferson both accepted this explanation.

The Albemarle farm proved less productive than Monroe had hoped. This was partly due to his own enthusiasm for politics. Monroe simply could not stay out of politics long enough to settle into a farmer's life.

State leaders in Richmond continued to encourage Monroe's political ambitions. In the fall of 1790, Monroe agreed to run for the U.S. Senate. He won the election easily. By November the Monroes were on the road to Philadelphia, the nation's temporary capital city.

CHAPTER THREE

A THANKLESS MISSION

You go, Sir, to France, to strengthen our friendship with that country. You will show our confidence in the French Republic.

—Secretary of State Edmund Randolph to James Monroe, June 1794

The leaders of the new U.S. government were people who had worked together to gain freedom from Great Britain. George Washington was president, John Adams vice president, Alexander Hamilton secretary of the treasury, and Thomas Jefferson secretary of state (previously called "foreign affairs").

But serious differences divided the leaders who had so recently been united against a common enemy. Washington, Adams, and Hamilton led a group that became known as the Federalist Party. The Federalists were known for their concern for and protection of the business classes. Their support was greatest in New England, home to many manufacturers and merchants. In foreign affairs, the Federalists favored Great Britain over France, because France was wracked by a violent revolution. Becoming involved in France's problems would not benefit U.S. businesses.

Jefferson and Madison (a member of the House of Representatives) opposed the Federalists. Their concern at home was for farmers, and in foreign affairs, they sympathized with the French revolutionaries. The U.S. Senate's newest thirty–two-year-old arrival, Senator Monroe, did not hesitate to join his two good friends.

When Monroe arrived in Philadelphia, he joined Jefferson and Madison in lodgings at a boardinghouse. (Elizabeth and Eliza went to New York to visit Elizabeth's family.) The three friends were united in their opposition to the Washington administration's Federalist-inspired policies. Together, they built a new political party, the Republicans, also known as the Democratic-Republicans.

SENATOR MONROE

The Senate had only twenty-six members in 1790, and unlike the House of Representatives, it held its sessions in secret. Senators met on the second floor of Congress Hall in Philadelphia, their chairs arranged in a circle. In cold weather, the senators huddled around the fireplace.

In this clublike setting, Monroe raised his objections to the Washington administration. Along with other Republicans, he opposed creating a Bank of the United States, believing it would favor business interests over farmers. He objected to the administration's choices for ambassadors to France and Great Britain, on the grounds that they were too pro-British.

Not all of Monroe's work in the Senate focused on the emerging political parties. Following a resolution passed by the Virginia legislature, Monroe proposed to open the Senate to public observation. This proposal drew strong opposition from senators who did not want an audience. Monroe persisted, however, and in 1794, the Senate changed its rules and opened its doors.

During adjournments of the Senate—breaks generally scheduled in spring and summer—Monroe and his wife and daughter returned to Virginia. Monroe added to his landholdings in Albemarle County by buying a large estate called Highland, just south of Jefferson's Monticello. Monroe looked forward to living at Highland. The farm grew wheat and tobacco, using slave labor. As in the past,

Before moving to Washington, D.C., in 1800, the Senate met in Congress Hall in Philadelphia (below).

A photograph of Highland, taken in the 1950s.

Monroe hoped the plantation would provide him with income to support his family.

But once again, politics interfered with Monroe's plans to become a Virginia planter. After completing his service as a senator in 1794, he left Philadelphia, but he was not bound for Highland. Monroe was going to France on behalf of President Washington—whose administration he had spent the past four years criticizing.

FRUSTRATION IN FRANCE

In the spring of 1794, Washington sent New Yorker John Jay to Great Britain. Jay's mission was to settle disputes with Great Britain relating to shipping and other claims. Jay was close to Hamilton, and both were pro-British Federalists.

To deflect criticism from Republicans and from the French government, Washington and his secretary of state, Edmund Randolph, decided to name a Republican as minister (ambassador) to France. They wanted a Republican whose tilt toward France was unquestionable. Monroe was their man.

Randolph and Washington gave Monroe specific written instructions before he left for Paris. Monroe was to "remove all jealousy with respect to Mr. Jay's mission" by assuring the French that the United States was not favoring Great Britain. He was also to assure the French that the United States would not weaken its ties with France. But he was to "insist upon compensation for the capture and spoliations of our property, and injuries to the persons of our citizens, by French cruisers [ships]," and to convince France to lift its restrictions on trade with the United States. In the final paragraph of the letter of instruction, Randolph concluded, "You will let it be seen, that in case of war, with any nation on earth, we shall consider France as our first and natural ally."

On June 18, 1794, Monroe, Elizabeth, and eight-year-old Eliza boarded a ship in Baltimore, Maryland, bound for France. The trip across the Atlantic Ocean took about one month, with pleasant sailing weather.

Soon after arriving in Paris, Monroe asked French leaders if he could address the National Convention, France's legislative body. The request was granted, and at two in the afternoon on August 14, 1794, the U.S. minister arrived to a cheering crowd outside the convention hall. Inside, before an audience of several hundred convention members, Monroe gave a warm, admiring speech.

Monroe addresses the French National Convention in 1794.

France and the United States, he said, "both cherish the same principles and rest on the same basis, the equal and unalienable rights of men." The new minister continued: "America had her day of oppression, difficulty and war, but her sons were virtuous and brave and the storm which long clouded her political horizon has passed and left them in the enjoyment of peace, liberty and independence." He complimented the French armed forces that were fighting the same sort of battle that American revolutionaries had won.

Monroe's French audience loved what he said. But Monroe's audience at home—namely, the Federalists who had sent him to France—did not like his speech at all. He was being far too friendly with his hosts. Washington had Randolph write a letter of disapproval to Monroe. The administration did not appreciate the "extreme glow" of parts of Monroe's speech, Randolph wrote. Moreover, when the administration had instructed Monroe to assure the French of the United States' loyalty, the assumption was that "your audience . . . would take place in the private chamber of some committee," not in full public view.

The letter did not reach Monroe until February 1795. For months he had little idea of the displeasure he had caused at home among the Federalists. He continued assuring France that the United States favored it over Great Britain. Even after he learned that he was out of step with the administration's views, Monroe continued in the same vein.

AT HOME ABROAD

Monroe found it difficult to toe the Federalist line in part because he simply liked France so much. The entire Monroe family felt comfortable in their host country. Eliza attended a prestigious Parisian school. Monroe and Elizabeth spoke French fluently. They enjoyed French food and art and adopted French fashions in clothing and furniture. The French affectionately called Elizabeth *la belle Americaine*—the beautiful American.

Monroe's ease with the French proved to be his undoing. The turning point came when Monroe learned that Jay had concluded a treaty with Great Britain in November 1794. The United States was anxious to avoid another war with Great Britain, and Britain knew it had this advantage in negotiating. As a result, Jay's Treaty gave Britain most of what it demanded. Monroe and many other Americans were outraged at this apparent show of favoritism toward the British. Jay's Treaty, he claimed, was "the most shameful transaction I have ever known of the kind."

Monroe received instructions from the administration on how he should explain Jay's Treaty to the French. He was to tell them that, despite the treaty, the United States was not anti-France. But Monroe largely disregarded these instructions. He followed his own heart and continued to speak against the treaty.

Washington could not tolerate an envoy who publicly spoke against U.S. policy. In June 1796, the new U.S. secretary of state, Timothy Pickering, sent Monroe a letter telling him that he had harmed the "justice, honor, and the faith of the country." After consulting with Washington, Pickering recalled Monroe from his post as minister to France.

If Monroe had been a Federalist, his recall could have ended his political career. Offending one's own party would leave a politician out in the cold. But Monroe was a Republican, and upon returning to the United States in June 1797, he found that he had the full support of his own party. Republicans were perfectly happy with Monroe's conduct. Even before he and his family got off the boat in Philadelphia, they received a visit from Jefferson, Aaron Burr, and Albert Gallatin—all active Republican leaders. They were there to welcome Monroe back to politics on this side of the Atlantic.

CHAPTER FOUR

GOVERNOR MONROE

It is unquestionably the most serious and formidable conspiracy we have ever known of the kind.

—James Monroe to Thomas Jefferson, describing a rebellion planned by Richmond slaves in the summer of 1800

Despite the warm welcome he received from his fellow Republicans, Monroe did not cheerfully settle into life as an ex-diplomat. He took criticisms of his conduct in France personally. Back in Virginia, Monroe was unable to let go of the feeling that the Federalists were wrong. Throughout the fall of 1797, Monroe worked furiously on a book that defended his actions.

The resulting five-hundred-page book, called *A View of the Conduct of the Executive, in the Foreign Affairs of the United States Connected with the Mission to the French Republic During the Years 1794, 5 & 6*, probably did not change any

During the presidency of John Adams (right), the conflict intensified over whether the United States should favor Britain or France.

minds about Monroe's conduct. Republicans basically agreed with Monroe, and Federalists did not. Jefferson called the work "masterly." The new president, John Adams, a Federalist, called Monroe a "disgraced minister, recalled in displeasure for misconduct." On hearing this, Monroe fumed in a letter to Madison about the "dishonorable & unmanly attack of our insane President."

Eventually, the furor over Monroe's mission to France died down, and he turned to other matters. First, he restarted his law practice to make some money. Second, Monroe worked closely with Jefferson and Madison on Republican Party affairs. The third matter that demanded Monroe's attention was Highland. While the Monroes were abroad, Jefferson had designed and started construction on the Monroe family's new house at Highland, but it was not yet ready. Finally, in May 1799, the family expanded with the birth of their second child, a son, James Spence.

Monroe could not keep his mind off politics, and his friends urged him to reenter public service. He considered running for the House of Representatives, the Senate, or the state legislature. Monroe's Republican friends in the Virginia Assembly made a different decision for him, however, when they elected him governor of Virginia in December 1799.

So it happened again: the politician in Monroe crowded out the planter. Ready to take up farming at his new plantation, Monroe had cleared more fields to increase crop production. The house at Highland was finally ready to be a home. The Monroes had moved their belongings there by the end of 1799, but the family was headed elsewhere. They had an appointment in Richmond, where Governor Monroe took office on December 19.

Under the Virginia constitution of 1776, the governor enjoyed prestige but little power. The assembly made most of the political decisions. Still, Monroe made the most of the office and proved himself an able administrator. He supervised the building of a state armory (a place where military equipment is stored) and a state-owned factory to produce guns and knives for the Virginia militia. He oversaw construction of a state prison. He paid careful attention to the appointment of officers to the courts and militia. He wrote detailed reports to the legislature and other officials.

GABRIEL'S REBELLION

All was not peaceful paper shuffling for Monroe. In the summer of 1800, Monroe and his family were on vacation at Highland. The Monroes' fifteen-month-old son had been sick with whooping cough and other ailments, including persistent fevers. His parents hoped the fresh country air would improve his health.

Monroe did not have the opportunity to help nurse his son. In August he had to return to Richmond to deal with an outbreak of yellow fever in the port city of Norfolk. As yellow fever was very contagious, Monroe ordered the quarantine of ships docked in Norfolk, preventing them from traveling to other ports in Virginia.

While Monroe was in Richmond, another threat arose: a potential slave revolt. Its leader was a slave named Gabriel, who lived on a plantation north of Richmond. Gabriel's owner was Thomas Prosser, one of the harshest slave owners in the area.

Gabriel was a talented carpenter and blacksmith, and he could read and write. He seemed, wrote a correspondent in the *Richmond Virginia Argus,* "a fellow of courage and intellect above his rank in life." Earlier that summer, Gabriel had begun organizing a revolt among local slaves. Gabriel was driven by anger toward his cruel owner but also by a belief in freedom. As one of Gabriel's top assistants in the planned revolt explained to another slave, "We have as much right to fight for our liberty as any men."

Gabriel's plan was bold. On August 30, the slaves would assemble. Some would set fire to Richmond's warehouses, while others would take over the state prison and kidnap Monroe. As the city burned, the slaves would murder white slaveholders.

But the plan was never carried out. Powerful thunderstorms swept through Richmond on August 30, washing out roads and bridges. While Gabriel and other slaves waited out the storm, slave owners found out about the rebellion. Monroe quickly called up the state militia, and a widespread search for the rebel slaves began.

These slaves are working on a plantation in the South. Field work is very strenuous, and slaves were often forced to labor in the field for twelve to sixteen hours per day.

As the slaves were caught, they were put on trial. Those slaves found guilty were hanged. Monroe was determined to stop the rebellion. But there were many slaves involved, and Monroe was troubled by the possibility of having to execute many men whose crime was plotting to fight for their freedom. He asked the Council of State to approve pardons for slaves not deeply involved in planning the revolt, but the council refused. Of approximately seventy men put on trial, forty-four were convicted and twenty-six were hanged. Gabriel Prosser was one of the last. He was captured on September 27, 1800, tried, convicted, and executed.

Monroe earned praise from Virginians for his handling of the slave uprising. But while Monroe dealt with his state's crisis, he faced a personal tragedy. His son, James Spence, could not shake the illnesses that had gripped him for months. On September 28, 1800, the little boy died.

CHAPTER FIVE

JEFFERSON'S MAN IN EUROPE

All eyes, all hopes are now fixed on you.

—President Thomas Jefferson to James Monroe, appointing him envoy extraordinary to France, January 13, 1803

Crushed by the death of her son, Elizabeth suffered poor health for months. Monroe also grieved deeply, but his work may have helped him through the tragedy. In the autumn of 1800, he took a leading role in guiding Republicans toward victories in elections for Congress, the presidency, and state legislatures. Jefferson became president. The Virginia legislature elected Monroe as governor two more times.

Monroe's third term as governor ended on December 24, 1802. His plan, once again, was to practice law, this time in Richmond. Three years of serving as a poorly paid governor had added to Monroe's money problems.

And with the birth of daughter Maria Hester, the family grew again to four members.

But in January 1803, Monroe received a letter from Jefferson that changed his plans. Jefferson wanted Monroe to go to France to help the U.S. minister, Robert Livingston. Livingston was negotiating with the French about American rights in the port city of New Orleans in the Louisiana Territory (land stretching from the Mississippi River to the Rocky Mountains). The president was not really asking Monroe to serve his country—he was telling him. By the time Jefferson put pen to paper to write his friend, he had already officially nominated Monroe as "envoy extraordinary" (special envoy) to France.

Jefferson had reasons for acting in such a bold manner. The situation on the American frontier needed urgent attention. The Louisiana Territory included the Mississippi River and most of the land west of the river to the Rocky Mountains. Control of the territory had been given to Spain by France in 1762. But as American settlers pushed farther west, they came to rely on using the Mississippi River freely, even though the river did not belong to the United States. Americans shipped their goods down the river and through New Orleans for sale to eastern states. Spanish forces tried to control use of the river, often clashing with American settlers. Then, in 1802, Spain suddenly announced that Americans no longer had the right to store goods in New Orleans. The withdrawal of this so-called right of deposit infuriated western Americans.

Unknown to the United States, Spain was planning to give control of the Louisiana Territory back to France. France and Spain agreed to keep their pact a secret. The

Napoleon Bonaparte's military campaigns against other European countries lasted for sixteen years, from 1799 to 1815. After 1803 he was particularly bent on destroying Great Britain.

ruler of France, Napoleon Bonaparte, wanted time to send troops to Louisiana to control American settlers.

Despite the attempt to keep the deal secret, rumors about it spread. Many Americans were unhappy at the idea of a French Louisiana. France had become a powerful nation. Napoleon had crowned himself emperor. His goal was to create a French empire with power over Europe—and over the North American lands controlled by France. Americans believed that France would try to limit use of the Mississippi River just as Spain had. Many westerners called for war against Spain and France.

Jefferson wanted to avoid war. In 1802, he and Madison, his secretary of state, had instructed Livingston to enter into talks with the French foreign minister, Charles-Maurice de Talleyrand-Perigord. Livingston asked the French either to acknowledge American rights to navigate the Mississippi River or to sell New Orleans to the United States. But Talleyrand would not even clearly admit that Spain was transferring Louisiana to France.

By January 1803, Livingston had been in France for more than a year with little to show for his efforts. People on the western frontier clamored for stronger action. Jefferson needed to show them that he was serious about their concerns. The best way to do that was to send someone to France who was known as a champion of the West. Monroe was the man for the job.

The president knew that his friend would understand the urgency and would not turn him down. "You possess the unlimited confidence of the administration and of the western people; and generally of the republicans everywhere; and were you to refuse to go, no other man can be found who does this," Jefferson wrote to Monroe. Monroe accepted.

THE LOUISIANA PURCHASE

In early March 1803, Monroe and his family left New York harbor in a snowstorm, bound for Europe. By April 12, they were in Paris. Little Maria Hester stayed at their Paris home with her mother. Eliza went to school. And the envoy extraordinary went to work, where Livingston met him with extraordinary news.

The day before Monroe arrived in Paris, Napoleon had renounced France's claim to Louisiana. "It is not only New Orleans that I cede," Napoleon had told his finance minister, "it is the whole colony, without reserve. I know the price of what I abandon. . . . I renounce it with the greatest regret; to attempt obstinately to retain it would be folly." Napoleon needed money and could not afford to continue protecting France's North American territory. He directed Talleyrand to negotiate a deal with Livingston. And so, on April 11, Talleyrand asked Livingston a question the American could not have predicted: would the United States be interested in buying not only New Orleans but all of Louisiana?

The Louisiana Territory was much larger than the present-day state of Louisiana. It covered nearly 830,000 square miles, from southern Canada to present-day New Mexico and from the Mississippi River to the Rocky Mountains. Neither Monroe nor Livingston had authority from their government to negotiate a purchase of this size. They could not confer quickly with their superiors at home, because communications across the Atlantic Ocean took months, and in the meantime, the French could withdraw the offer.

Monroe (left) *and Livingston* (center) *finalize the Louisiana Purchase with Foreign Minister Talleyrand* (right). *The Louisiana Purchase remains the largest area of territory ever added to the United States at one time.*

Despite their lack of authority, Monroe and Livingston pressed forward. The opportunity was simply too good to pass up. They negotiated a price of $15,000,000—$11,250,000 for the land itself, plus $3,750,000 to be paid to American businesses that had claims against the French. The United States bought the Louisiana Territory for three cents per acre. The deal was signed on May 2, 1803, and approved by the U.S. Senate on October 20.

Whether Monroe's presence was important to the transaction that doubled the size of the United States is uncertain. The Louisiana Purchase may have occurred without him. But the fact that Monroe participated in the deal was important to his reputation as a national leader. By August 1803, Jefferson had appointed Monroe to the important position of U.S. minister to Great Britain.

ON TO SPAIN

The Louisiana Purchase treaty left unclear the exact location of the territory's boundaries. The treaty didn't mention the region known as "the Floridas" (present-day Florida). This did not stop Americans from concluding that West Florida was part of Louisiana and, therefore, part of the United States. (Spain assumed it held both West and East Florida.)

Jefferson knew that Spain might not share the U.S. conclusion. The U.S. minister to Spain, Charles Pinckney, urged the Spanish to agree that West Florida was part of the United States. Spain vigorously refused. Madison, as secretary of state, turned to Monroe in London for help. Madison wrote to Monroe on October 26, 1804, asking him to travel immediately to Madrid, the Spanish capital.

Monroe arrived in Madrid in January 1805. But like Pinckney, he had no success changing the views of the Spanish government. He left Madrid in the summer of 1805, his mission a failure.

BACK TO BRITAIN

Monroe and his family returned to London in late July 1805. He turned to another difficult assignment from the Jefferson administration. He was supposed to negotiate a treaty that would stop Great Britain's abusive treatment of American ships and sailors at sea.

Relations between Great Britain and its former colony were seriously strained. The United States was caught in the middle of the conflict between Great Britain. Each European power enacted laws to try to force the United States and other countries to trade only with it. In enforcing these laws, Great Britain stopped American ships at sea, seized their cargoes, and blockaded ports so that ships could not enter or leave freely. British warships patrolled U.S. coasts and threatened American ships. Great Britain also declared that American ships would not be permitted to carry goods produced in French and Spanish colonies to Great Britain. As trade from these colonies was a profitable part of the U.S. shipping industry, this declaration made many Americans angry.

Great Britain had another policy that Americans found offensive—impressment. Under impressment, the British forcibly boarded American ships and arrested sailors they claimed were British subjects. Those sailors were then forced to serve in the British navy. Great Britain said that it meant only to impress sailors who were British subjects. Americans insisted that the British were impressing U.S. citizens.

Impressment was an emotional issue for many Americans. Relations with their former ruler were already strained, and Britain's abusive treatment of American ships only made matters worse.

Monroe's instructions were to convince the British to stop impressments and to allow U.S. ships to once again carry cargoes from the French and Spanish colonies. Months passed, and Monroe's negotiations with British officials stalled. Jefferson sent a second envoy to help Monroe, Baltimore lawyer William Pinkney. The two U.S. envoys were unable to budge the British from their positions on the most important issues dividing the two nations.

Great Britain's arguments had some persuasive power. Napoleon posed a tremendous threat. To have any hope of repelling him, Britain's navy had to be at full strength, even if that meant gaining sailors through impressments. And Britain's tight limits on trading with its enemy were designed to cause economic problems for Napoleon's growing empire.

Under these circumstances, Monroe and Pinkney decided to depart from their instructions. In December 1806, they signed a treaty that did not require the British to pay for illegally seizing American ships. It did not reverse British restrictions on shipments of enemy colonial cargoes, but it did loosen the rules somewhat. Perhaps most important, the treaty made no mention of impressments. Instead, in a side note, the British government asserted that it had a "right" to impress British sailors but "that the strictest care shall be taken to preserve the citizens of the United States from any molestation [disturbance] or injury."

William Pinkney

From Monroe and Pinkney's point of view, this was the best deal the United States could get. The two envoys sent a messenger with the treaty, along with a detailed letter of explanation, to Madison on January 3, 1807. The next step would be for Jefferson to approve the treaty and send it to the Senate for ratification.

Before Monroe and Pinkney's messenger reached Washington, D.C., however, the British minister there received his own copy of the treaty, which he gave to Madison. When Madison and Jefferson saw that the document lacked a provision on impressments, they decided it was unacceptable. Jefferson refused even to send the pact to the Senate for consideration.

Word of Jefferson and Madison's abrupt rejection reached Monroe in London. That his old friends should dismiss the fruits of his hard work out of hand—without even reading his explanation—hurt Monroe deeply. Jefferson assured Monroe that the criticism was not personal. But the president made clear his distaste for the treaty: "The British commissioners appear . . . to have taken everything, and yielded [given up] nothing."

HOME TO VIRGINIA

Monroe and his family left London in November 1807. The journey home was plagued by bad weather. By the time the Monroes reached Virginia on December 13, 1807, they were exhausted and sick.

Monroe also suffered from another malady: resentment. Although he believed that Jefferson meant no harm, he thought Madison had treated him wrongly. To Monroe it seemed Madison intended to make him look bad and to eliminate him as a political rival in the 1808 presidential election.

With these troubling thoughts, Monroe traveled to Washington, D.C., only a few days after arriving home. He expected Jefferson and Madison to ask him to participate in discussions about the diplomatic crisis with Britain. After all, Jefferson had confirmed their friendship in a letter. But when they did not include Monroe in their talks, his suspicions about Madison were confirmed. Sorely disappointed in his friends and in his party, he went home to Highland to tend to his plantation—and to his future.

CHAPTER SIX

SEASONED LEADER

War, dreadful as the alternative is, could not do us more injury than the present state of things, and it would certainly be more honorable to the nation, and gratifying to the publick feelings.

—James Monroe, autumn 1811

Monroe had been away almost five years, serving Jefferson and his country. During that time, some members of the Republican Party had grown apart from the Jefferson-Madison leadership. Those members formed a faction (a group with an opinion differing from the majority) that included some Virginians, such as the outspoken John Randolph. The faction was angered by how the Jefferson administration was handling international trade issues. They were particularly angry about the Embargo Act of 1807, which temporarily halted all trade in and out of U.S. ports. This caused considerable economic distress among southern planters, who wanted to sell their crops in Europe.

The disgruntled Republicans knew that Madison, Jefferson's secretary of state, was the favored Republican candidate for president in 1808. They wanted to send a message that he was not everybody's favorite. Randolph and others had been urging Monroe, through letters sent to him in London, to challenge Madison. Monroe had always turned away from such talk, wishing to maintain party unity. But after being slighted by Jefferson and Madison, he was ready to listen. He agreed to run against Madison.

Although Monroe allowed the Republican faction to put his name in the race, he did not really campaign. His supporters published letters promoting him, but Monroe did not criticize Madison. His campaign was more of a protest than a grab for the presidency.

On Election Day in November 1808, Madison soundly defeated Monroe and other candidates to become the fourth president. Monroe accepted Madison's victory without question and looked forward to serving in the new administration. Given his past relationship with Madison, Jefferson, and the Republican Party, Monroe expected a major role in Madison's cabinet, such as secretary of state. After Madison's election, Monroe waited to hear from him. But no letter came from the new president.

HOME LIFE

With his public life in decline, Monroe turned to his family and home. The Highland plantation required attention. Monroe was interested in winemaking, and he imported grapevines from France with the idea of developing a vineyard. Monroe also inherited property in Loudoun County, Virginia, when his uncle Joseph died in 1808. That plantation, called Oak Hill, demanded Monroe's time as he retreated into his private life.

In September 1808, the Monroes hosted Eliza's wedding at Highland. Eliza married George Hay, a lawyer active in Virginia's Republican affairs. The following year, the Hays had a baby girl, Hortensia. The Monroes' younger daughter, Maria Hester, loved her older sister's new baby, and Hortensia loved her six-year-old aunt Maria.

Monroe enjoyed life at Highland. He experimented with different methods of farming. He rode horses and hunted. He often visited Jefferson at Monticello. And Monroe spent more time with Elizabeth. The two were devoted to each other and talked about everything from home furnishings to politics—sometimes in French.

BACK IN THE GAME

Jefferson was determined to heal the bad feelings between Madison and Monroe. Madison, too, wanted to end the falling out. He thought Monroe might want to serve as governor of the Louisiana Territory. Jefferson carried this offer to his neighbor. "The sum of his answers," Jefferson wrote to Madison on November 30, 1809, "was that to accept of that office was incompatible with the respect he owed himself; that he would never act in any office where he should be subordinate to any but the President himself. . . ." In other words, Monroe was only interested in a cabinet position.

Although he insisted on only the highest-level appointment in the national government, Monroe did not decline other offices in state government. In 1810 he won election to the Virginia House of Delegates for the third time. In his campaign, he declared his loyalty to the established

Republican Party, putting distance between himself and those who had championed him for president in 1808. Monroe and Madison publicly restored their friendship in May 1810, when Monroe traveled to Washington and had a cordial meeting with the president.

In January 1811, the Virginia legislature elected Monroe as governor. Monroe's election signaled that he was back in the good graces of Virginia Republicans loyal to Jefferson and Madison. Three months into his governorship, in March 1811, Monroe's return to the Jefferson-Madison fold was completed when Madison sought his help. In the continuing conflict between France and Great Britain, Madison had proclaimed the United States neutral, but in practice his administration favored France. In doing so, Madison made war with Great Britain appear nearly certain. Secretary of State Robert Smith was not up to the job of handling the ongoing crises in foreign affairs. Madison wanted—finally—Monroe as secretary of state.

The prize he desired was his, but Monroe did not grab it immediately. He wanted to be sure that, as a cabinet member, he would be able to speak his mind. Madison assured Monroe that he welcomed fresh ideas and that peace with Great Britain was not out of the question. With these assurances, Monroe accepted the position.

The Monroes moved to the nation's capital in the spring of 1811. Washington, D.C., was hardly yet a city. Pigs roamed the unpaved streets, and there were few impressive buildings. The Monroes lived rather modestly, although they often entertained guests. Their home at Highland was too far away for frequent visits. However, their inherited plantation,

Oak Hill, was only thirty miles away from the capital, and they went there when they wanted to escape the city.

WAR AGAIN

The new secretary of state faced old problems. Great Britain continued to interfere with U.S. trade and continued to impress American sailors. Monroe tried to keep negotiations open with British ministers. But he also kept in close contact with Congress's pro-war faction, called the "war hawks." Representatives and senators from the South and West tended to favor fighting Great Britain. Federalist Party members and northerners were generally more pro-British and opposed to war.

The war hawks' complaints against Great Britain went beyond trade and impressments. Some believed the British in Canada incited Native Americans to attack U.S. citizens on

Some Native Americans resented the westward movement of U.S. citizens and began to attack settlements in the Great Lakes region.

the frontier and around the Great Lakes. They wanted to stop these attacks and even dreamed of winning Canada from the British. Another group saw war as an opportunity finally to take West Florida from Spain, an ally of Great Britain.

For a while, Monroe hoped for a peaceful conclusion to the disputes. Great Britain indicated it would ease its restrictions on U.S. shipping. It would not, however, stop impressments. In contrast to his position in 1806, Monroe was no longer willing to compromise on this. He and other U.S. officials sought respect from Great Britain, not simply freedom of the seas.

The buildup to a military conflict was unstoppable. On June 1, 1812, Madison asked Congress for a formal declaration of war. By mid-June, Congress acted and the nation was at war, once again, with Great Britain.

Monroe agreed with the decision to go to war. He was, in fact, itching to get into the war personally. Just as when he was a teenaged Revolutionary War officer, the fifty-four-year-old secretary of state sought a war command. He urged Madison to put him in command of the invasion of Canada, but Madison wanted Monroe in Washington. The secretary of war, William Eustis, was totally overwhelmed. In December 1812, Eustis resigned, and Madison replaced him with Monroe.

Monroe's leadership skills made an immediate impact on the War Department and on war planning. He created supply systems, improved communications, and worked closely with the military committees of Congress. He wrote a plan for the invasion of Canada.

But Madison had appointed Monroe secretary of war on an "acting," or temporary, basis. In February 1813, Madison chose John Armstrong of New York as permanent secretary of war, in part because so much of the fighting was taking place in that state. Monroe continued in his position as secretary of state.

DOWNWARD SPIRAL

The war was not going well for the United States. The army lacked soldiers. Land battles were nearly all disasters. Although U.S. warships performed well, they were outnumbered by the British fleet. British ships sailed freely on the Chesapeake Bay and, in July 1813, appeared at the mouth of the Potomac River. Monroe feared an attack on Washington, D.C., and urged the president to reinforce the capital's defenses. He also wanted to establish a group of express riders (scouts on horseback) whose job would be to report on enemy movements throughout the Chesapeake region. But Armstrong did not share Monroe's concerns, and Madison chose to follow the advice of his chief war planner, not his chief diplomat.

This lack of concern toward the British threat proved nearly fatal to the nation's capital. In the summer of 1814, British ships massed at the Potomac's mouth. This time, Madison sent Monroe to lead an outfit of soldiers on a scouting mission. On August 20, they found British troops about to march overland to the capital. At the same time, British ships were sailing up the Potomac toward Washington.

Monroe worked without rest to keep up with British movements. But the capital had lost its chance to defend itself. On August 24, the British invaded Washington after first defeating U.S. forces in Bladensburg, Maryland. By the time the enemy soldiers marched into the city, most of its citizens were already gone. Monroe was among the last government officials to leave.

The British set fire to the city. It was saved from total destruction only by powerful rainstorms that night. The storms put out the flames and drove the British from the conquered capital. By August 27, Monroe was back in the blackened city, accompanying Madison to survey the damage.

British troops set fire to many U.S. government buildings, including the Capitol, the president's house, and the offices of the Department of State.

The Madisons and the Monroes stayed in the Octagon House (above, photographed in the early 1900s) *while Washington was rebuilt.*

A DOUBLE SECRETARY

The devastation of Washington, D.C., turned Madison against the ineffective Armstrong. By September, Armstrong was forced out of office. Madison once again appointed Monroe to the position. Monroe was both secretary of war and secretary of state.

He turned his immediate attention to the defense of Baltimore. Monroe created the communications system he had wanted to build the year before. He tried to increase the number of U.S. troops by raising their salaries. He was not entirely successful, because Congress still would not commit the resources needed to wage a full-scale war. But the Americans did manage to drive the

British troops pounded Baltimore's Fort McHenry with rockets and bombs through the night of September 13, 1814. The attack failed, inspiring Washington lawyer Francis Scott Key to write the "Star-Spangled Banner."

British away from Baltimore in mid-September and also won victories on Lake Champlain and the Great Lakes. During this time, Monroe "never went to bed," he wrote. "I had a couch in a room in my house on which I occasionally reposed [rested], but from which even in the night, I was called every two hours, when the expresses arrived, to receive the intelligence which they brought, & to act on it."

While Monroe worked to keep the United States in the fight in the summer of 1814, U.S. and British negotiators began to meet in Ghent, Belgium, to discuss settlement of the disputes between the two nations. But the negotiations did not go well for the U.S. side. Great Britain had defeated Napoleon and could turn all its attention to war with the United States. In this position, the British were not eager to compromise. According to the U.S. negotiators, peace would be possible only if the United States stopped insisting that a treaty must end British impressments.

By then what had been nonnegotiable to Madison and other Republicans for years became negotiable. Finally, the president agreed that the U.S. negotiators could ignore the impressment issue. Monroe sent word of this change to the Americans in Ghent in October 1814. This was, of course, the position Monroe had taken in 1806 when he signed the treaty with Great Britain that Madison and Jefferson had rejected. And this was the position that led to a peace treaty between the United States and Great Britain on Christmas Eve 1814.

Word of the treaty traveled across the Atlantic Ocean as quickly as it could, but not quickly enough to prevent one more battle. On January 8, 1815, 7,500 British soldiers attacked 6,000 Americans at New Orleans. Led by General Andrew Jackson, the Americans drove the British from the port city at the mouth of the Mississippi. Jackson and his men also took over western Florida from Spanish forces. The Battle of New Orleans was a spectacular victory for the United States. News of the triumph reached the nation's capital in mid-February—the same time that the capital's residents learned of the treaty. The war was over.

The Treaty of Ghent, as the peace pact was called, did little more than restore prewar relations between the two

U.S. and British representatives sign the Treaty of Ghent, which ended the War of 1812, on Christmas Eve 1814.

countries. The shipping issues that had led to the war were not settled, but few Americans complained. They were relieved that a disorganized conflict that could have torn apart the nation was over.

PATRIOT'S REWARD

Monroe was so exhausted that many who saw him assumed he was ill. In March 1815, he resigned as secretary of war, keeping his post as secretary of state. He and Elizabeth went to the countryside so that he could regain his strength. By October 1815, he was well and returned to Washington.

Madison was nearing the end of his second term in office. After his outstanding service in Madison's cabinet, Monroe was ready to become president, and the country was ready to elect him. Not even his most serious challenger for the post, William Crawford of Georgia, put up much of a fight. In the spring of 1816, the Republicans in Congress chose Monroe over Crawford to be their party's presidential candidate in the fall election. They selected Daniel Tompkins of New York as the party's vice presidential candidate.

The Federalist Party had largely collapsed after its opposition to the War of 1812. The dying party entered a presidential candidate, Senator Rufus King of New York, but there was no contest. Monroe won decisively.

Monroe won the 1816 presidential election by a landslide.

CHAPTER SEVEN

THE FIFTH PRESIDENT

If we look to the history of other nations, ancient or modern, we find no example of a growth so rapid, so gigantic, of a people so prosperous and happy.

—James Monroe, first inaugural address, March 4, 1817

March 4, 1817, was an unusually warm day in Washington, D.C. People turned out in droves for the inauguration of the fifth president of the United States. The ceremony took place outside, so the pleasant weather was fortunate. But it was not the thermometer that had guided the Senate inaugural committee in planning the nation's first open-air presidential inauguration.

Past presidents had taken their oaths of office in the House of Representatives chamber, but this year Speaker of the House Henry Clay was feeling uncooperative. He and Senate committee members had been quarreling over the

Monroe's inauguration was the first presidential inauguration held outdoors. An enthusiastic crowd attended the celebration.

details of furniture arrangements for the inauguration. Clay's irritation probably had more to do with his being passed over by Monroe for secretary of state. Whatever the precise reason, he refused to allow the inauguration to take place in the House of Representatives.

On a platform erected in front of the Capitol Building, Monroe stood before a crowd of about eight thousand. In some ways, Monroe was a throwback to an earlier time. He still wore knee breeches and silk stockings, a cocked hat and a sword, although these so-called "small clothes" were no longer the fashion. At fifty-nine, he had deep lines in his face and gray hair, but he still appeared strong and tall.

Shortly after noon, Monroe delivered his inaugural address. He was not an inspiring speaker, and it is doubtful that many actually heard his words. Still, he discussed plans for his presidency in some detail. National defense was a top priority. The new president believed that the War of 1812 had taught the nation that it must have sufficient armed forces to call its own. The United States should not rely on state militias. "Our land and naval forces should be moderate," he said, "but adequate to the necessary purposes."

Monroe closed his speech with grand patriotic sentiments. In his view, the U.S. government "approached to perfection," and "in respect to it we have no essential improvement to make." With these happy thoughts, Monroe became president.

GOING ON TOUR

The president's mansion was still under repair from damage done by the British attack of 1814, so the Monroes did not move there after the inauguration. Instead, the family left Washington before the summer. Elizabeth and Maria headed southwest to Oak Hill. Monroe traveled northeast.

The new president wanted to tour the country, starting with the northeastern states. His stated purpose was to visit forts, shipyards, and other installations relating to the nation's military defense. But Monroe also saw the opportunity to create a sense of unity throughout the country. With the Federalist Party fading away, he hoped to usher in a time of political harmony.

As Monroe set out on his grand tour on May 31, 1817, he attracted criticism. George Washington was the only president who had taken such a journey, and some thought Monroe

Monroe was the first president since George Washington to tour the country.

should not try to follow in the footsteps of "the father of the country." But the critics' voices were soon drowned out. The president traveled by carriage, by steamboat, and on horseback. He went from Baltimore to Philadelphia to New York to the cities of New England. Admiring crowds came out to see and hear him. People seemed genuinely to like the formal but friendly and simple man who was their president.

A Boston, Massachusetts, newspaper, the *Columbian Centinel*, predicted that the president's tour was the start of an "era of good feelings" for the United States. This type of sentiment followed Monroe wherever he went during his fifteen-week trip. By the time he returned to Washington, D.C., on September 17, he had traveled three thousand miles.

"THE ERA OF GOOD FEELINGS"

For many, feeling good about their president was easy. The end of the War of 1812 marked the beginning of a time of productivity, optimism, and patriotism in the United States. Many felt proud that the young nation had stood up to the older European powers. In the East, new and improved inventions increased the output of products ranging from cloth to iron. In the South, cotton production soared. Settlers were pushing farther west for land, adventure, and fortune.

Monroe's selections for his cabinet reflected his interest in promoting harmony. He brought together talented people from different regions, with many points of view. For secretary of state, he chose John Quincy Adams of Massachusetts, an experienced statesman and son of former president John Adams. Monroe asked his Republican rival for the presidency, William Crawford, to be secretary of treasury. John

Monroe and his cabinet (from left to right): *John Quincy Adams, William Crawford, William Wirt, Monroe, John Calhoun, Daniel Tompkins, and John McLean.*

Calhoun was secretary of war. For attorney general, Monroe selected a respected Virginia lawyer, William Wirt.

Beneath the surface of the era of good feelings, however, some troubles simmered. Social and political divisions between southern and northern states were increasing. Cotton had become the chief crop of the South, and the slave labor that supported the cotton industry was the basis of the South's economy. But at the same time, support for laws that would abolish slavery was growing in the North.

The nation's economy was also not entirely sound. The banking system was just getting started, and the value of money was variable. This created uncertainty about the prices of some goods and the value of property. Also, not all of the nation's banks were experienced in managing the money people entrusted to them.

But in the fall of 1817, as the Monroes moved into the newly restored president's mansion—which everyone would soon be calling the White House, for its freshly white-washed exterior—these issues did not cloud the horizon of what looked like a bright future for the United States.

SECURING BORDERS

The exact boundary line of that U.S. horizon was unsettled as Monroe's presidency began. Monroe supervised negotiations over the nation's northern boundary with Canada, a British territory. Under the Rush-Bagot Treaty of 1817, the United States and Great Britain agreed to keep only a small number of armed ships on the Great Lakes to limit expensive and dangerous military competition in the region.

The two countries then signed the Treaty of 1818. That drew the boundary between the United States and Canada at the forty-ninth line of latitude, stretching across the North American continent. Only competing claims to Oregon, which negotiators left for another day, prevented the boundary line from reaching all the way to the Pacific Ocean.

In the South, the United States had taken over West Florida during the War of 1812. But Spain held East Florida, and it became a haven for runaway slaves from Georgia, Alabama, and South Carolina. In Spanish Florida, the slaves joined the Seminole and other Native Americans driven by U.S. soldiers from their lands in Georgia. The Native Americans, sometimes with help from the former slaves, launched raids on U.S. settlers in Georgia.

Monroe felt he had to act to stop these attacks. In December 1817, he instructed General Andrew Jackson to take command of U.S. troops in the troubled region. As the president told members of Congress in January 1818, Jackson was only to cross into Spanish Florida if necessary to pursue attacking Seminoles. Once there, the general was to withdraw as soon as possible. Jackson's orders, Monroe assured Congress, required him to recognize Spanish authority in Florida.

Jackson had different ideas. Commanding his own volunteer militia from Tennessee, he invaded Spanish Florida in the spring of 1818. Jackson and his troops destroyed Native American villages and executed tribal leaders. On April 7, the troops took over the Spanish fort at Saint Marks, and in May they attacked Pensacola, forcing the Spanish governor and soldiers to flee to Cuba.

Jackson had gone beyond Monroe's instructions, but he insisted his actions were necessary to establish security on the nation's southern border. For Monroe, Jackson's actions presented a problem—but also an opportunity. The problem

Though General Jackson overstepped his boundaries by invading Pensacola, his victory there presented an opportunity to expand the United States.

was political. By invading Spanish Florida, Jackson treaded on the president's authority and on Congress's power to declare war. Accepting Jackson's actions would also worsen relations with Spain and could even lead to war.

The opportunity presented by Jackson's victories in Florida was geographical. Spain was incapable of controlling Florida. Jackson's presence there suggested that the United States might finally take over the southern edge of the country all the way to the ocean.

With the help of John Quincy Adams, Monroe carved out a response that solved the problem and took advantage of the opportunity. The president did not severely criticize his general, but he did agree to give Spain back its two forts. At the same time, Adams pressed the Spanish minister to the United States, Luis de Onis, to clearly spell out Florida's future. By

February 1819, Adams and Onis agreed that all of Florida belonged to the United States. For this land, the United States paid five million dollars and recognized Spanish ownership of Texas. The two nations also agreed on a line between their territories in the western part of the North American continent, all the way to the Pacific Ocean. The Senate immediately ratified the Adams-Onis Treaty, or Transcontinental Treaty. Sixteen years after he had signed the Louisiana Purchase as envoy extraordinary to France, Monroe presided over the final settlement of the Louisiana Territory's borders.

THE PANIC OF 1819

The nation's borders were more certain than at any time in its history. Inside those borders, however, uncertainty was growing. In his annual address to Congress in December 1818, Monroe stated that "commerce has flourished, the revenue has exceeded the most favorable anticipation," but these cheerful observations were outdated even as he wrote them.

Prices for farm products and manufactured goods were dropping. For example, cotton that farmers sold for thirty-three cents per pound in 1818 was bringing only eighteen cents per pound by the fall of 1819. Banks were loaning less money. The value of land was sinking fast. By the spring of 1819, the nation was experiencing its first economic depression (downturn).

As a result of the economic downturn, businesses failed and workers lost jobs. In Philadelphia, for example, three-quarters of the workforce had no jobs. Many people could not pay their bills or make purchases. The results of the depression, called the Panic of 1819, were plain to see—suffering families, bankrupt businesses, and idle factories.

How the "Monroe" got in Monrovia

Why is the capital of a country in West Africa named after James Monroe? James Monroe owned slaves nearly all his life, but he also favored the gradual end of slavery in the United States. Like other southerners who thought that slavery had to cease, Monroe believed that abolition (making slavery illegal) had to take place over time. To free slaves all at once, he feared, would result in violence and could tear the country apart.

Other white and free black Americans had been talking since the early 1700s about creating a separate territory for blacks. Whether within or outside the United States, the territory would be someplace for freed slaves and other free blacks to settle. Opinions about this idea differed widely. Some people, black and white, found the notion completely racist. It was, they said, simply a way of ridding the United States of blacks rather than giving them equal rights. Others, also black and white, embraced the idea, arguing that black people would never gain equal rights in the United States, so they should form their own country.

In 1800, during Monroe's first term as governor of Virginia, he faced Gabriel's Rebellion, a well-organized revolt planned by Richmond slaves. Although the revolt was never carried out and caused no deaths, Virginia courts sentenced twenty-six rebel slaves to death. Of the harsh sentences, Monroe wrote, it was "difficult to say whether mercy or severity was the better policy in this case, tho' when there is cause for doubt, it is best to incline to the former policy," that is, to mercy.

The harsh outcome of Gabriel's Rebellion spurred Monroe to explore the idea of sending rebel slaves, as well as other blacks, to a foreign country. In 1801 he and Jefferson began to discuss the creation of a colony for black people. Among other

Joseph Jenkins Roberts was the first black president of independent Liberia. He served from 1847 until 1856. Like many early U.S. leaders, Roberts was born in Virginia.

possibilities, they considered establishing a settlement on the west coast of Africa.

Fifteen years later, Monroe was elected president. Just after his election, in December 1816, a group of influential white men formed the American Colonization Society in Washington, D.C. The society's purpose was "to promote and execute a plan for colonizing (with their consent) the Free People of Color residing in our Country, in Africa, or such other place as Congress shall deem most expedient."

Monroe was a strong supporter of the society. In 1819 Congress authorized Monroe to give $100,000 to the group for purchase of land in Africa. In December 1821, the society bought land in West Africa from local leaders. In 1822 the society established a colony there called Liberia, which means "freedom." Society leaders named the colony's capital Monrovia, to honor Monroe.

Liberia was never really a U.S. colony. The United States did not claim to rule it, and in 1847 Liberia declared itself an independent country. Enthusiasm for the colonization idea fizzled out only a few years after Liberia's creation. Opponents of slavery and black people themselves opposed kicking freed slaves out of the country. By the end of the 1800s, between twelve thousand and twenty thousand blacks had moved to Liberia—only a tiny fraction of the U.S. black population.

Monroe and other policymakers lacked good ideas about how to turn the economy around. Monroe and others urged people to work harder and spend less. The federal government allowed people who had bought federal lands on credit to delay their payment for several years. But for the most part, the Panic of 1819 was allowed simply to run its course.

SLAVERY AND THE MISSOURI COMPROMISE

Neither Monroe nor Congress could allow the other major crisis that arose in 1819 simply to run its course. This was the disagreement between North and South over the question of slavery in the Missouri Territory (the land of present-day Missouri).

The Missouri Territory, which allowed slavery, had applied to become a new state of the Union. At first, the application seemed like a routine matter. But it soon came to reveal a much larger issue.

Northern representatives in Congress wanted to prevent slavery from spreading into new states. They also argued that admitting Missouri as a slave state would create a political imbalance in Congress. The country had eleven slave states and eleven free states. The admission of Missouri as a slave state would tilt the balance in favor of southern states. Southerners countered with the argument that each state should be able to choose or reject slavery itself. And they argued that outlawing slavery in Missouri would tilt the balance in Congress in favor of the North.

By the time Congress met again in December 1819, the nation was in an uproar over Missouri. Monroe was deeply concerned. "I have never known a question so menacing to the tranquility and even the continuance of our Union as the present one," he wrote to Jefferson on February 19, 1820.

Monroe did not believe that the federal government had the right under the Constitution to tell a state whether it should allow slavery. Despite this opinion, Monroe did not take a central role in the debate on the Missouri question, and he did not lead the way to a solution. He was not by nature a man of big ideas and striking leadership. Besides his own personality and limitations, however, Monroe was held back by the traditions of his day. The early presidents usually did not interfere with workings and debates of Congress, and Monroe did not break new ground.

Fortunately, Congress had leaders of its own who labored through the Missouri crisis. Despite talk of splitting the nation in two, a compromise emerged in March 1820. Missouri joined the Union without any restriction on its right to permit slavery. This move was balanced by the admission of the new state of Maine, which prohibited slavery. The remainder of the Louisiana Purchase—out of which Missouri had been carved—was divided into free and slave sections. The Missouri Compromise patched up the division between North and South, at least for the time being.

CHAPTER EIGHT

TIMES OF CHANGE

[T]he American continents, by the free and independent condition which they have assumed and maintain, are henceforth not to be considered as subjects for future colonization by any European powers.

—James Monroe to Congress, December 1823

The anger surrounding the Missouri crisis did not boil over into the presidential election of 1820. No Republicans emerged to challenge Monroe for his party's nomination to run for a second term. As for what remained of the Federalist Party, it did not put forth a candidate at all.

Monroe won a majority in every state in the voting in December 1820. His second inauguration ceremony was held on March 5, 1821. The cold rain and sleet in the nation's capital that day could not have been more different from the balmy sunshine that graced Monroe's first inauguration. But bad weather did not discourage thousands of

This print shows the U.S. Marine Corps Band standing in front of the White House.

people from crowding inside and outside the House of Representatives, where the ceremony took place.

The House chamber was newly decorated with red upholstered chairs and gold curtains. It also had a distinct echo that made most speakers, including the president, impossible to hear. After Monroe took the oath of office, the U.S. Marine Corps Band performed, starting a tradition that has been unbroken ever since. Then President and Mrs. Monroe received guests at the White House. At an inaugural ball held that evening at Brown's Hotel, the Monroes left early—not even staying for dinner.

PRESIDENCY, MONROE-STYLE

Leaving the guests at his own inaugural ball was perfectly in keeping with Monroe's presidential style. He and his wife and family conducted themselves in the White House as they wanted to, not necessarily as others might have wished. From their years in Europe, Monroe and Elizabeth had developed formal ways. They decorated the White House with elegant furniture and silverware they had bought in France. Although their taste in decorating attracted admiration, their formal manners drew complaints. Monroe put more limits than previous presidents on meetings, receptions, and dinners, which caused some dissatisfaction among members of Congress and of his administration. But it was Elizabeth who caused the greatest uproar.

Elizabeth knew how to entertain, but she chose to limit her socializing. She was frequently ill, but even when healthy, she often just wanted to be left alone. Unlike her

Elizabeth Monroe drew criticism for not holding frequent lavish receptions. Many Washingtonians felt she was being snobbish by not socializing with them.

predecessor as First Lady, Dolley Madison, Elizabeth did not visit the wife of every diplomat and member of Congress who came to town. When people made social calls at the White House, Elizabeth frequently was absent, sending Eliza to represent her. (Eliza and George Hay lived at the White House, as George was a close adviser to the president.) Eliza was not only formal, but she could also be arrogant and rude. None of this endeared the Monroe women to Washington society.

The Monroes did not help matters when they hosted the first White House wedding. Their younger daughter Maria married New Yorker Samuel Gouverneur. In planning the wedding, Elizabeth kept the guest list small and private, despite pressure from outsiders to throw a large party. She did not respond to repeated requests from diplomats for a longer guest list. Instead, she asked Secretary of State Adams to tell the diplomatic corps to leave her alone.

GOOD-BYE TO "GOOD FEELINGS"

While some Washingtonians suffered hard feelings over Elizabeth's social style, the nation at large was losing the "good feelings" that had marked the president's first term. Differences between North and South were growing, despite the recent Missouri Compromise. Personal rivalries among the nation's leading politicians also changed Monroe's second term for the worse. Three of his cabinet members—Secretary of Treasury William Crawford, Secretary of State John Quincy Adams, and Secretary of War John Calhoun—hoped to become president in the 1824 election. Andrew Jackson and Speaker of the House Henry Clay were also in the race.

"Queen Elizabeth"

Maybe it was her upbringing as the little girl of a wealthy, well-known New York family that made Elizabeth Kortright Monroe *(below)* behave in a manner that many observers found haughty. Maybe it was her frequent and mysterious illnesses that caused her to withdraw from the public, sparking complaints that she was a snob and rumors that she drank alcohol to excess. (She may have suffered from epilepsy, about which little was known at the time and which would explain her unpredictable fainting spells.) Whatever the exact reason, Elizabeth both fascinated and disappointed many members of Washington society with her aloofness. He was President Monroe, but she was—in comments passed behind her back—"Queen Elizabeth."

Elizabeth did look the part of the queen. She was beautiful and graceful. She wore expensive dresses of French design that one might have seen in a royal court in Europe. The First Lady and president also redecorated the White House in the fashion of the royal courts of Europe, and their dinners were served in a formal style.

But Elizabeth did not hold enough dinners, formal or otherwise, to satisfy Washington society. She also left the capital frequently to visit family. This put a crimp in

Washington social life, as women generally did not attend White House functions in the absence of a hostess. Elizabeth's standoffishness caused "no little mortification and disappointment [among the] ladies," a senator from Massachusetts wrote home. On the rare occasion when Elizabeth gave a White House party, the wives of congressmen were apt to stay away, in retaliation for her refusal to pay social calls on them. "The drawing room of the President was opened last night," one woman wrote in December 1819, "to a beggarly row of empty chairs. . . . Only five females attended, three of whom were foreigners."

Elizabeth often had her grown daughter, Eliza, stand in for her at official events. This solved the problem of men-only gatherings at the White House but created new controversy. Washingtonians found Eliza as haughty as her mother and not particularly nice. On one occasion, she did not wish to reveal the whereabouts of her husband George to people outside the family. Nonetheless, they persisted in asking where he was, until she responded sarcastically, "He is dead. And I'll hear nothing more of it."

Despite the criticism, Elizabeth may have performed a service for all the presidents' wives who came after her. Before Elizabeth, Dolley Madison had made it a habit to visit practically every official's wife who came to the nation's capital. This was a difficult task even in her time and would have become a punishing burden as Congress and the rest of official Washington expanded. There were simply too many people and too few hours. Elizabeth set an example for future First Ladies who wished to keep some things private and who wanted to take charge of their own schedules and lives.

Competition among these presidential hopefuls and their supporters was so intense that it interfered with the administration's ability to set policy. For example, when Adams presented the Senate with a treaty between the United States and Great Britain to limit international trading in slaves, Crawford's Senate allies voted against it. As a result of the scheming and rivalries surrounding his ambitious cabinet members and their supporters, Monroe's influence as chief executive was seriously strained. Days after the start of Monroe's second term, Clay told Adams that although the president had been elected nearly unanimously, "he had not the slightest influence in Congress."

THE MONROE DOCTRINE

Amid these political problems at home, Monroe faced a foreign policy challenge that called for decisive action. In South and Central America (also called Latin America), several of Spain's former colonies had revolted. They declared their independence as the new nations of Mexico, Argentina, Chile, and Colombia. Many Americans favored the independence of these new republics, and Monroe granted them official U.S. recognition.

In contrast, the European powers of France, Austria, Russia, and Prussia (part of modern-day Germany) were interested in helping Spain win back its Latin American colonies and in stopping further revolutions. Great Britain's position was more in tune with the U.S. point of view. It welcomed the opportunity to engage in trade with independent Latin American countries, and it wanted to prevent other European powers from interfering with the new governments. To further this interest, the British minister to the

United States, Stratford Canning, wanted the two countries to issue a joint statement warning Europe not to try to intervene in Latin America.

Canning's proposal reached Washington in October 1823. The idea of joining with Great Britain, which was still a great naval power, had some appeal to Monroe and other Americans. The United States' military power was not strong enough to hold off European forces on its own. Monroe favored taking a stand against the anti-independence European powers because, as he wrote to former president Madison, if those nations invaded the former colonies, "they would, in the next instance, invade us."

Madison favored joining in a British statement. So did Jefferson. Monroe respected the opinions of his two friends and former presidents. However, he and Secretary of State Adams were anxious not to make the United States appear inferior to Great Britain. Adams also urged Monroe to consider the separate threat posed by Russia. That nation, which possessed land in present-day Alaska, was extending its claims down the Pacific Coast.

After lengthy meetings with his cabinet and with Adams's encouragement, Monroe decided not to join in a British statement. Instead, in his annual message to Congress on December 2, 1823, the president announced a new U.S. policy. The United States, Monroe said, would view as unacceptable any European interference in the affairs of the independent Latin American countries. At the same time, the United States pledged not to interfere with the remaining European colonies in the Western Hemisphere. To signal to Russia that it should not try to extend its control down the Pacific Coast, Monroe also pronounced the Western

In this political cartoon, Uncle Sam (right, *representing the United States) draws a line in the sand, warning other nations not to invade U.S. territory.*

Hemisphere closed to further European colonization. Years later, the president's pronouncement became known as the Monroe Doctrine.

Across the United States, Americans were pleased with the president's declaration. Some expressed doubts at the ability of the nation to follow through on Monroe's muscular tone, given the weakness of the nation's defenses and armed forces. The European powers also knew that the United States lacked the strength to back up its words. But since Great Britain separately opposed European intervention in Latin America, the other powers refrained from mischief. As for the Pacific Coast, in 1824 Russia gave up its claims to land south of the line that later became the Alaska border.

GROWING PAINS

The Monroe Doctrine reflected the idea, still new and bold at the time, that the United States was destined to stretch from the Atlantic Ocean to the Pacific Ocean. Americans had begun their westward movement with the Louisiana Purchase, so that by 1820, 25 percent of the country's population lived west of the Appalachian Mountains.

For the people who settled in the West, one of the most pressing needs was the construction of roads, bridges, and canals—known as "internal improvements." Without decent transportation, cotton grown in the South could not make its way to the northern mills that wove it into cloth. Clothing and shoes manufactured in the Northeast needed to be shipped to customers in the South and West.

From his own travels and experience, Monroe understood the need for transportation projects to tie the nation together. But he still subscribed to the old-fashioned Republican idea that the Constitution created a federal government of limited powers that was prohibited from constructing internal improvements. He was willing to enlarge the federal government's power—but only by adding an amendment (formal change) to the U.S. Constitution.

Monroe's positions on internal improvements were not entirely rigid, however, and in 1824 he signed the Survey Act, providing for a large-scale mapping of the country's geographical features and property boundaries. Creating these maps was a necessary step in planning for a national system of roads and canals. In this way, Monroe put the nation on the road toward a general program of internal improvements, even while he kept to his view that such a scheme was not within the constitutional powers of the national government.

THE 1824 ELECTION

Monroe's final year in office, 1824, was unpleasant for him. The politics of the 1824 presidential election were bitter and personal, and prevented much real work from getting done in the federal government. Even after Election Day, the race was not over. Andrew Jackson won

This political cartoon satirized the 1824 presidential election. In it, the election is conceived of as an actual foot race, with Adams leading the race.

the greatest number of popular votes. But in the final vote that determined the presidency—ballots cast by each state's representatives to the Electoral College—no candidate received sufficient votes to claim victory. According to the rules of the Constitution, the election went to the House of Representatives for a decision.

To avoid the appearance that he favored any side, Monroe decided not to appoint people to government positions until after the House voted on the next president. This decision angered treasury secretary and candidate Crawford, who had hoped the president would appoint some of his friends to federal jobs. Crawford came to Monroe to insist on action. "I wish you would not dilly-dally about it any longer," he told the president, "but have some mind of your own and decide it so that I may not be tormented with your want of decision." When Monroe responded by demanding whether Crawford had come to the White House to insult him, Crawford raised his walking stick. "You infernal scoundrel," Crawford said. Monroe raised his own weapon—a pair of metal fireplace tongs—and ordered Crawford to leave the room. Before the incident went any further, Crawford calmed down and apologized. The president and the man who hoped to become president then shook hands.

But Crawford did not win the election. On February 9, 1825, as a snowstorm blew through the capital, the House of Representatives elected John Quincy Adams the sixth president of the United States.

CHAPTER NINE

WINDING DOWN

His life for the last six years has been one of abject penury and distress, and they have brought him to a premature grave.

—diary of John Quincy Adams, on the death of James Monroe

Monroe and Adams had gotten along well, and Monroe was pleased to turn over the presidency to him on March 4, 1825. The Monroes returned to Oak Hill, where they easily fell into the routines of rural life. Eliza and George also spent most of their time at Oak Hill, with their daughter Hortensia.

Monroe concerned himself with his plantation's output—wool from his flock of several hundred sheep, wheat, and rye. He kept in close correspondence with Jefferson and Madison and saw both frequently. Retirement also gave the former president time to enjoy horseback riding and visiting with friends.

The Monroes were happy to return to their peaceful estate at Oak Hill, where they remained until 1830.

MONEY TROUBLES

Like Jefferson, who died in 1826, Monroe was burdened by significant debts after a lifetime in politics and government service. He sold the Highland plantation for a disappointing amount. The money was not enough to cover his debts. Monroe turned to Congress for payment for thirty years of public service, going back to his first mission to France, from 1794 to 1797.

Many members of Congress were unwilling to give Monroe the tens of thousands of dollars he claimed. They did not want to set an example for other officials to follow. In addition, Monroe had made enemies in Congress during the last election. Despite this opposition, Monroe worked patiently at pressing his claims, writing documents and gathering evidence. Congress finally voted to give him nearly thirty thousand dollars in 1826 and another thirty thousand dollars in 1831. This was less than what Monroe felt he was due, but it did help him get out of debt.

CLOSING DAYS

In late 1828, Monroe suffered a serious fall while horseback riding, and his health declined. Still, in October 1829, he traveled to Richmond to participate in the Virginia Constitutional Convention. Madison was also there, and Monroe was delighted to work once again with his friend.

Eliza accompanied him to Richmond because of his weaknesses. Monroe's failing health was apparent, as his once-strong body and full face were both very thin. He worked on the convention's business until December 1829, when illness got the best of him. Monroe returned to Oak Hill, where he attended to farm business and his accounts with Congress. He also began an autobiography, which he never completed.

In September 1830, Monroe was devastated by two personal tragedies. First, George died suddenly, leaving Eliza a widow. Then, only days later, Elizabeth died on September 23. In a letter to a friend who had also recently lost his wife, Monroe mourned, "We have both suffered, the most afflicting calamity that can befall us in this life."

After Elizabeth's death, Monroe moved to New York City to live with Maria and her family. By the spring of 1831, he had developed a constant cough. Monroe was so sick he could barely write to his old friend Madison. On July 4, 1831, Monroe died in New York City at the age of seventy-three. He was the third president to die on Independence Day, after John Adams and Jefferson, both of whom had died exactly five years earlier.

LEGACY

In death, Monroe received the respect and reverence he had sought during his life. Thousands marched in his funeral procession in New York City. Around the country, communities stopped their daily business to listen to church bells ringing in his memory and to speeches praising him. President Andrew Jackson, who had succeeded John Quincy Adams in 1829, declared a special military day of honor for the former president.

Monroe was buried in Hollywood Cemetery in Richmond, Virginia.

In newspapers and in speeches, Americans remembered Monroe mostly as a hero of the American Revolution. His service in the Confederation Congress and the Senate, as a foreign emissary, a Virginia governor, a cabinet member, and even as president did not draw great praise. In later years, too, historians have not credited Monroe with contributing a great deal to the nation's development, except for his announcement of the Monroe Doctrine, which later presidents used as a basis for U.S. policies in the Western Hemisphere.

Monroe was not a bold leader. In the crises of his presidency, such as the Panic of 1819 and the Missouri Compromise, he let others take the lead. In foreign affairs, his secretary of state, John Quincy Adams, shaped many decisions of the U.S. government. In his service in London, Paris, and Madrid, Monroe did not so much shape events as he did follow and react to them.

Yet Monroe displayed bravery and boldness as a soldier in the American Revolution. During the War of 1812, he also demonstrated tremendous energy and leadership in the face of danger. And although William Wirt, Monroe's attorney general, described Monroe's mind as "neither rapid nor rich," two of the nation's most rapid and rich minds—Thomas Jefferson and James Madison—counted him as their close friend.

Jefferson and Madison, like many other men of the time, probably appreciated Monroe's patriotism, friendliness, and capacity for hard work. Even Wirt admitted that what Monroe lacked in brilliance, he made up for "with a judgment strong and clear, and a habit of application which no difficulties can shake, no labours can tire." And in a comment that was frequently repeated even during Monroe's lifetime, Jefferson reflected on Monroe's honesty when he wrote, "Turn his soul wrong side outwards and there is not a speck on it."

Monroe may have been exactly the president Americans demanded and deserved when they elected him to two terms in office. People seemed to want a president who reminded them of their recent victories to become and stay an independent nation. Perhaps Americans did not want their president to have firm ideas about how to address the new challenges of the emerging nation. They chose instead one who listened to many points of view. Like his nation, Monroe had one foot in the past and the other stepping—with many uncertainties and quite a few missteps—into the future.

TIMELINE

1758 James Monroe is born on April 28 in Westmoreland County, Virginia.

1774 Monroe enrolls in the College of William and Mary in Williamsburg, Virginia.

1775 The Revolutionary War begins in April. Seventeen-year-old Monroe volunteers in a Virginia infantry regiment.

1776 The Continental Congress adopts the Declaration of Independence on July 4. Monroe and his regiment join General George Washington's Continental Army in New York. Monroe fights in Battles of Harlem Heights, White Plains, and Trenton. He is seriously wounded in the Battle of Trenton.

1777 Monroe fights in the Battles of Brandywine Creek and Germantown, Pennsylvania, and spends the winter at Valley Forge with Washington's army.

1778 Monroe serves in the Battle of Monmouth and as a scout for General Washington.

1780 Governor Thomas Jefferson of Virginia accepts Monroe as a law student.

1781 With the surrender of the British at Yorktown, Virginia, the Revolutionary War ends. The new nation, the United States of America, is organized under the Articles of Confederation.

1782 Virginians elect Monroe to the Virginia House of Delegates.

1783 The House of Delegates elects Monroe to represent Virginia in the Confederation Congress. He serves for three years.

1786 On February 16, Monroe marries Elizabeth Kortright of New York. The couple moves to Fredericksburg, Virginia, where Monroe practices law. Daughter Eliza is born in December.

1787 Monroe is elected again to Virginia's House of Delegates.

1788 Monroe votes against ratifying the Constitution proposed by the Philadelphia Convention of 1787. The Constitution is approved despite his vote. Monroe runs for a seat in the new U.S. House of Representatives. He loses to James Madison.

1790 Monroe is elected to the U.S. Senate and moves to the temporary capital in Philadelphia.

1794 President George Washington appoints Monroe U.S. minister to France. The Monroes arrive in Paris in the summer.

1799 In May the Monroes' second child, James Spence, is born. In December, Monroe is elected governor of Virginia.

1800 Gabriel's Rebellion, a slave revolt, is discovered and thwarted. James Spence dies.

1803 Maria Hester, a second daughter, is born. Monroe participates in negotiating the Louisiana Purchase with France. Jefferson appoints Monroe U.S. minister to Great Britain.

1808 Monroe runs for president against Madison and loses.

1810 Monroe is elected again to the Virginia House of Delegates.

1811 Monroe is elected as governor again but serves only three months, as he accepts Madison's appointment as secretary of state. The Monroes move to Washington, D.C.

1812 The War of 1812 between the United States and Great Britain begins.

1814 The British invade Washington, D.C. Madison appoints Monroe secretary of war in addition to his post as secretary of state. On December 24, U.S. and British negotiators sign a peace treaty ending the war.

1816 Monroe is elected fifth president of the United States.

1817 Monroe goes on an extensive tour of the nation.

1819 Monroe's secretary of state, John Quincy Adams, concludes a treaty with Spain that gives Florida to the United States. The nation experiences its first economic depression.

1820 The Missouri Compromise settles the dispute over slavery in states carved out of the western territories. Monroe is elected to a second presidential term. Maria Hester marries Samuel Gouverneur in the first wedding ever held at the White House.

1823 In his annual message to Congress, Monroe says that the United States will no longer permit European interference in the Western Hemisphere. This announcement becomes known as the Monroe Doctrine.

1825 John Quincy Adams becomes the sixth president. The Monroes retire to their estate at Oak Hill in Loudoun County, Virginia.

1831 Monroe dies on July 4, becoming the third president to die on the anniversary of the nation's independence.

Source Notes

7 Michael K. Ward, "The Federalist Period, 1789–1800," *Lecture Pages in U.S. History,* 2002, <http://home.att.net/~history240/history100federalistsandjeffersonians.html> (July 19, 2004).

11 George Washington, *The Writings of George Washington,* ed. John C. Fitzpatrick (Washington, DC: Government Printing Office, 1936).

16 Harry Ammon, *James Monroe: The Quest for National Identity* (New York: McGraw–Hill, 1971), 6.

19 W. P. Cresson, *James Monroe* (Chapel Hill: University of North Carolina, 1946), 28.

23 Thomas Jefferson, *The Papers of Thomas Jefferson,* Avalon Project at Yale Law School, 1996–2000, <http://www.yale.edu/lawweb/avalon/jefflett/let18.htm> (May 13, 2004).

25 James Monroe, *The Writings of James Monroe,* ed. Stanislaus Murray Hamilton (New York: G. P. Putnam's Sons, 1898), 1:39.

26 John N. Pearce, "James Madison and James Monroe," Remarks presented at The James Madison Museum, Orange, Virginia, September 25, 1991, <http://www.jmu.edu/madison/center/main_pages/madison_archives/life/presidency/monroe.htm> (May 27, 2004).

27 Monroe, *The Writings of James Monroe,* 7:233–234.

27 Ibid., 231–233.

28–29 Ibid., 169.

30 Ibid., 173.

33 Ibid., 199.

34 Edmund Randolph, *The Writings of James Monroe,* 2:8.

38 Ibid., 3.

38 Ibid., 6.

38 Ibid., 8.

39 Monroe, "Address to the National Convention," August 14, 1794, *The Writings of James Monroe,* 2:13.

39 Ibid.

40 Stanley Elkins and Eric McKitrick, *The Age of Federalism* (New York: Oxford University Press, 1993), 499.

40 David C. Whitney and Robin Vaughn Whitney, *The American Presidents* (Pleasantville, NY: Reader's Digest, 1985), 50.

41 Ammon, 151.

42 Monroe, *The Writings of James Monroe,* 3:208.

43 Ammon, 167.

43 Ibid., 168.

43 Monroe, *The Writings of James Monroe,* 3:136.

45 Susan DeFord, "Gabriel's Rebellion," *Washington Post,* February 6, 2000, F1.

45 Ibid.

47 Thomas Jefferson, *Thomas Jefferson: Letters 1760–1826,* Jefferson Digital Archive, University of Virginia Archive, n.d., <http://etext.virginia.edu/jefferson/texts/> (February 23, 2004).

50 Ibid.

50 Henry Adams, *History of the United States of America during the Administrations of Thomas Jefferson* (New York: Library of America, 1986), 320.

55 Ammon, 260–261.

56 Ibid., 266.

57 Monroe, *Writings of James Monroe,* 5:191.

59 Ammon, 280.

66 Cresson, 275.

71 James Monroe, "First Inaugural Address," *The Papers of James Monroe,* Avalon Project at Yale Law School, 2004, <http://www.yale.edu/lawweb/avalon/presiden/inaug/monroe1.htm> (July 2, 2004).

73 Ibid.

73 Ibid.

74 "James Monroe," *The American President*, Miller Center for Public Affairs, University of Virginia, 2004, <http://www.americanpresident.org/history/jamesmonroe/> (May 27, 2004).

79 Noble E. Cunningham, Jr., *The Presidency of James Monroe* (Lawrence: University Press of Kansas, 1996), 81.

80 "James Monroe and Slavery," Ash Lawn–Highland Museum Home Page, 2004, <http://www.ashlawnhighland.org/jm—slavery.htm> (May 13, 2004).

81 Henry Noble Sherwood, "The Formation of the American Colonization Society," *Journal of Negro History*, vol. 2 (July 1917), repr. in *Documenting the American South* (Chapel Hill: University of North Carolina, 2000), <http://docsouth.unc.edu/church/sherwood/sherwood.html> (May 13, 2004).

82–83 Cunningham, 102.

84 Monroe, "Monroe Doctrine," *The Papers of James Monroe*, Avalon Project at Yale Law School, 2004, <http://www.yale.edu/lawweb/avalon/monroe.htm> (May 27, 2004).

89 Betty Boyd Caroli, *First Ladies* (New York: Oxford University Press, 1987), 18.

89 Ibid., 19.

89 Carl Sferrazza Anthony, *America's First Families* (New York: Simon & Schuster, 2000), 95.

90 Cunningham, 127.

91 Ibid., 153.

95 Ammon, 543.

95 Ibid., 544.

96 Whitney and Whitney, 54.

98 Ammon, 569.

100 Eugene Scheel, "Loudoun Author's New Book Illuminates Financial Struggles of James Monroe," *Washington Post*, July 15, 2001, T03.

100 Ibid.

101 Thomas Jefferson, *The Papers of Thomas Jefferson*, ed. P. Boyd (Princeton, NJ: Princeton University Press, 1955), 11:97.

Selected Bibliography

Ammon, Harry. "James Monroe," *Encyclopedia Americana Online.* 2004. <http://ap.grolier.com/article?assetid=0275240–00&templatename=/article/article.html> (July 19, 2004).

———. *James Monroe: The Quest for National Identity.* New York: McGraw-Hill, 1971.

Caroli, Betty Boyd. *First Ladies.* New York: Oxford University Press, 1987.

Cresson, W. P. *James Monroe.* Chapel Hill: University of North Carolina Press, 1946.

Cunningham, Noble E., Jr. *The Presidency of James Monroe.* Lawrence: University Press of Kansas, 1996.

DeFord, Susan. "Gabriel's Rebellion." *Washington Post,* February 6, 2000, F1.

Malone, Dumas. *Jefferson and His Time: The Sage of Monticello.* New York: Little Brown, 1981.

Monroe, James. *The Papers of James Monroe.* Avalon Project at Yale Law School. 2004. <www.yale.edu/lawweb/avalon/presiden/monroepa.htm> (July 19, 2004).

———. *The Writings of James Monroe.* Edited by Stanislaus Murray Hamilton. 7 vols. New York: G. P. Putnam Sons, 1898–1901.

Pearce, John N. "James Madison and James Monroe." Remarks presented at the James Madison Museum, Orange, Virginia, September 25, 1991. 2004. <http://www.jmu.edu/madison/center/main_pages/madison_archives/life/presidency/monroe.htm> (July 19, 2004).

Whitney, David C., and Robin Vaughn Whitney. *The American Presidents.* Pleasantville, NY: Reader's Digest, 1985.

Wiltse, Charles M. *The New Nation, 1800–1845.* New York: Hill and Wang, 1961.

FURTHER READING AND WEBSITES

Behrman, Carol H. *Thomas Jefferson*. Minneapolis: Lerner Publications Company, 2004.

Beschloss, Michael, ed. *American Heritage Illustrated History of the Presidents.* New York: Crown Publishers, 2000.

Bohannon, Lisa Frederiksen. *The American Revolution.* Minneapolis: Lerner Publications Company, 2004.

Bowen, Andy Russell. *The Back of Beyond: A Story about Lewis and Clark*. Minneapolis: Carolrhoda Books, Inc., 1997.

Childress, Diana. *The War of 1812.* Minneapolis: Lerner Publications Company, 2004.

Corrick, James A. *The Louisiana Purchase.* San Diego: Lucent Books, 2001.

"Elizabeth Kortright Monroe." The White House. <http://www.whitehouse.gov/history/firstladies/em5.html>. The White House's official website features biographies of the First Ladies of the United States, including Elizabeth Monroe.

Fitz-Gerald, Christine Maloney. *James Monroe.* Chicago: Children's Press, 1987.

Gaines, Ann Graham. *James Monroe, Our Fifth President.* Chanhassen, MN: The Child's World, Inc., 2002.

Hakim, Joy. *The New Nation*. New York: Oxford University Press, 2002.

"James Monroe." *The American President.* Miller Center for Public Affairs, University of Virginia. <http://www.americanpresident.org/history/jamesmonroe/>. This detailed website covers Monroe's entire life and includes links to other sites of interest.

"James Monroe." *The Internet Public Library.* <http://www.ipl.org/ref/POTUS/jmonroe.html>. The Internet Public Library features general biographical information, interesting facts about Monroe, and links to Monroe's inaugural addresses.

"James Monroe." *The White House.* <http://www.whitehouse.gov/history/presidents/jm5.html>. The White House's official biography focuses on Monroe's presidency in historical context.

The James Monroe Museum and Memorial Library. <http://www.mwc.edu/jmmu/>. Highlights of the site include biographical articles on Monroe's life and presidency and photographs of Monroe family furnishings and personal possessions.

McPherson, Stephanie Sammartino. *Liberty or Death: A Story about Patrick Henry.* Minneapolis: Carolrhoda Books, Inc., 2003.

Miller, Brandon Marie. *Growing Up in Revolution and the New Nation.* Minneapolis: Lerner Publications Company, 2003.

Mitchell, Barbara. *Father of the Constitution: A Story about James Madison.* Minneapolis: Carolrhoda Books, Inc., 2004.

Roberts, Jeremy. *James Madison.* Minneapolis: Lerner Publications Company, 2004.

INDEX

About the Author

Debbie Levy earned a bachelor's degree in government and foreign affairs from the University of Virginia, as well as a law degree and master's degree in world politics from the University of Michigan. She practiced law with a large Washington, D.C., law firm and worked as a newspaper editor. Her previous books include *Lyndon B. Johnson*, *John Quincy Adams*, and *The Vietnam War*. Levy enjoys paddling around in kayaks and canoes and fishing in the Chesapeake Bay region. She lives with her husband and their two sons in Maryland.

Photo Acknowledgments

The images in this book are used with the permission of: The White House, pp. 1, 7, 11, 23, 34, 42, 47, 57, 71, 84, 96; Dictionary of American Portraits, p. 2; Library of Congress, pp. 6 [LC-USZ62-16956], 14, [LC-USZC4-4600], 26 (right) [LC-USZC4-4098], 29 [LC-USZ62-113385], 31 [LC-USZC4-2541], 32 [LC-D416-9861], 36 [HABS,PA,51-PHILA,6A-28], 65 [LC-USZ62-104119], 70 [LC-USZ62-117118], 81 [LC-USZC4-4609], 85 [POS-TH-MUS, no.8], 86 [LC-USZ62-99130], 88 [LC-USZ62-113384], 94 [LC-USZ62-89572], 99 [LC-USZ62-73820]; © Stock Montage, Inc., pp. 12, 74; © North Wind Picture Archives, pp. 16, 54; National Archives, pp. 20 [W&C #31], 43, 64 [NWDNS-111-SC-96969], 68 [NWDNS-111-SC-96965]; Independence National Historic Park, p. 26 (left); © Lee Snider/CORBIS, p. 30; © Getty Images, p. 37 © Picture History, p. 39 © Historypictures.com, p. 46 © Independent Picture Service, pp. 49, 55; © Bettmann/CORBIS, pp. 51, 61, 72, 75, 92; Courtesy Chicago Historical Society, p. 66; © CORBIS, p. 78; Library of Virginia, p. 97.

Cover: © Stock Montage, Inc.